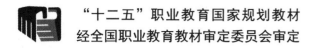

"十二五"职业教育国家规划教材
经全国职业教育教材审定委员会审定

A New English Course for Business Studies

—Writing Skills

新商务英语写作教程

主　　编：张东昌　李淑琼

副 主 编：潘巍巍　陈卫红

清华大学出版社
北　京

内 容 简 介

《新商务英语写作教程》为专业核心课教材，全书共 16 个单元，精心设计的任务型活动贯穿每个教学单元，每单元由 Learning Objectives, Warming-up Activities, Sample Study & Writing Tips, Vocabulary in Use, Practical Writing Tasks 和 Key Sentences for Reference 6 个模块构成，组织和安排多层次、多种形式的写作训练活动，对学生的英语写作技能进行训练。

本教材可供应用型本科和高职高专院校商务英语专业及应用英语专业外贸和涉外文秘方向的学生使用。

图书在版编目（CIP）数据

新商务英语写作教程 / 张东昌，李淑琼主编. —北京：清华大学出版社，2015（2023.3重印）
新商务英语教程
ISBN 978-7-302-39545-4

I. ①新… II. ①张… ②李… III. ①商务-英语-写作-教材 IV. ①H315

中国版本图书馆CIP数据核字（2015）第039675号

责任编辑：赵洛育
装帧设计：张　宇
责任校对：赵丽杰
责任印制：沈　露

出版发行：清华大学出版社
　　　　　网　　　址：http://www.tup.com.cn，http://www.wqbook.com
　　　　　地　　　址：北京清华大学学研大厦 A 座　　　邮　　编：100084
　　　　　社 总 机：010-83470000　　　　　　　邮　　购：010-62786544
　　　　　投稿与读者服务：010-62776969，c-service@tup.tsinghua.edu.cn
　　　　　质量反馈：010-62772015，zhiliang@tup.tsinghua.edu.cn

印 装 者：三河市龙大印装有限公司
经　　销：全国新华书店
开　　本：185mm×260mm　　　　印　张：13　　　字　数：324 千字
版　　次：2015 年 7 月第 1 版　　　印　次：2023 年 3 月第 10 次印刷
定　　价：48.80 元

产品编号：053689-02

　　《新商务英语写作教程》的编写力求使学生掌握商务英语写作的基本知识，提高学生的商务英语写作能力，培养高校英语专业、商务英语专业和相关专业复合型国际商务人才。

　　本教材的编写力求真实地反映国际商务所涉及的主要活动和环节，语言材料经过精选，重视材料的真实性、新颖性、规范性和实用性，注重训练国际商务活动中的各种相关语言表达方式和方法，崇尚任务型教学的理念，按以学生为中心的教学模式编写，让学生在任务中体验做中学、学中做，实战实训，学以致用。

　　本教材共分为 16 个单元，每单元讲授 4 学时，每学期学习 8 单元，分两个学期授完。

　　新商务英语写作教程每单元主要包括以下几个模块：

Learning Objectives（本单元学习目标）

Part I　Warming-up Activities　（与本单元写作主题相关的热身活动，其中包括与单元写作主题相关的商务知识阅读材料）

Part II　Sample Study & Writing Tips（与本单元写作主题相关的实用写作范文讲解和训练以及写作指导）

Part III　Vocabulary in Use　（与本单元写作主题相关的词汇、表达方式及注释）

Part IV　Practical Writing Tasks（本单元写作主题实战训练）

Part V　Key Sentences for Reference（与本单元写作主题相关的经典必备例句）

　　本教材由张东昌、李淑琼担任主编，负责全书的策划、拟定大纲及统稿总撰；由潘巍巍、陈卫红担任副主编。

　　在编写本教材的过程中参考了大量的相关教材和书籍以及网上资料，在此对所有作者表示衷心的感谢。

　　本教材的编写得到了杨亚军教授、谢职安教授的指导，在此表示衷心的感谢。

　　由于编者水平有限和编写时间仓促，书中难免有错误之处，敬请读者不吝赐教，以便今后进一步修改完善。

编　者

2014 年 7 月

目 录

An Overview of
Business English Writing

Learning Objectives

To be proficient in

➢ understanding useful words and expressions used in this unit;
➢ knowing the functions, types, principles and formats of business writing;
➢ learning the design of an elegant letter head, a standardized inside address and a perfect letter body.

Part I　Warming-up Activities

Task 1

Read the following passage and tell the formats of business letter.

Business Letter is an important part of the business activities through email and other communicative styles. There are many communicative types in business activities, say, business memo, notice, advertisement, telegram, fax, invitation, emails etc. Generally speaking, a business letter includes: letterhead, inside address, salutation, body, complimentary close, and signature.

Letterhead refers to the addresser's address and the date of writing the letter. They may be positioned at the center or at the left margin of the top of the page, including your address, telephone number, E-mail and date. The date is usually placed two lines below the addresser's information. It is usually shown in the order day/month/year (English Practice) or month/day/year (American Practice). The date should always be typed in full and should not be abbreviated.

Inside Address gives the full name, title and the address of the receiver, typed on the left corner of the letter one or two lines below the writer's address and the date, is printed as it will appear on the envelope.

Salutation is placed at the left margin two lines below the inside address and two lines above the body of the letter. Generally speaking, we use "Dear+Mr.\Miss.\Ms.+surname" if we know his or her name. Otherwise, we often use Dear Sir/Madam.

Body customarily consists of three paragraphs. The first paragraph acts as an introduction or an acknowledgement of the previous correspondence. The middle part usually discusses matters or gives information. The last paragraph expresses a hope.

Complimentary close is simply a polite way to end a letter. The complimentary close of the letter should be coherent with the salutation. It appears either in the middle of the page or starts at the left-hand margin, two lines below the closing sentence. For examples: *Yours faithfully/Faithfully yours.*

Signature is located at the end of the letter, whether it is typed or not. The typed name can be placed four lines below the complimentary close, and the handwritten one can signed between. The formal letter without signature not only shows no respect to the reader, but also becomes invalid.

Task 2

Work in pairs and write down the key elements involved in business writing according to the following conversation.

A: Can you help me for a minute?

B: Sure, what can I do for you?

A: I'm trying to write a letter to one of our clients, but I just don't know what exactly to say.

B: For a start, you can just put Dear Sir or Madam, officially not personally.

A: OK, I first thank them for their business, so I can say something like "we are very grateful for your continuing support", How is that?

B: Good! But also, you have to tell them the reason of your writing, give them more reference.

A: Like "Regarding our new product line, we would like to announce a special price discount".

B: Right, do you need them to respond?

A: Yes, the letter would have a survey inside, and they should complete it and return to our office. How should I write that?

B: You can tell them "Please find the enclosed customer service survey", else also, " Please return the survey at your earliest convenience."

B: Great! What do you think I should close it with?

A: Since you don't know them that well personally, probably the best way is "your sincerely", also say "Best Regards".

B: OK, thanks a lot for your help!

Task 3

Work in pairs or groups to discuss the following questions.

1. What should you pay attention to when writing a letterhead?
2. How do you place salutation in business writing?
3. How many parts are involved in the body of business writing?
4. Why is signature necessary in the formal business letter?

Part II   Sample Study & Writing Tips

 # Sample 1 Formats of business letter

Intel Labs China
No.2 Kexueyuan South Street, Haidian District, Beijing
Tel: 010-8529-8800 Fax: 010-8529-8801

May 20,2012
Zhou Na
16 College Way
Oregon city, OR 26768

Dear Miss Zhou,

I wish to acknowledge receipt of your order for 100,000,000 pieces of cells. I've already sent my assistant, Yu Hua, to deal with your order and she will give you a reply as soon as everything is arranged.

I'm looking forward to doing further business with you.

Yours Sincerely,
Cao Yin

Writing Tips

Consideration is put in the first place, which means to put yourself in his or her place, and give consideration to his or her wishes, demands, interests and difficulties. Try to find the best way to express your better understanding and present the message.

Task 1

Regarding the principle of consideration, please compare the following examples to see which expression is more appropriate for business writing.

1. We allow 2 percent discount for cash payment.
2. You earn 2 percent discount when you pay cash.
3. We won't be able to send you the assistant this month.
4. We will send you the assistant next month.

Sample 2 Requesting the change of order

Dear Mr. Brown,

Re: New Product Advertisement Booking

Thank you for your letter of 12 April 2014 concerning our new product advertisement booking. I am writing to inform you that certain changes have been made because we have increased the budget on the advertising campaign.

We need to change the following details. Firstly, we would like to book color page adverts instead of black and white. In addition, we would like our adverts to appear in four issues rather than two, that is, June, July, August and September. Finally, I would be grateful if you could quote us a new price and offer us a 10% discount considering the large number of issues in which we place the adverts.

I am sorry for any inconvenience this has caused and look forward to your early reply.

Yours sincerely
Thomas Davis

Writing Tips

Consideration is usually preferred in writing a business letter, which implies the letter should be specific, definite rather than vague, abstract and general. Take, for example, some qualities or characters of goods that should be shown with exact figures and avoid words like short, long or good.

Also *clarity* is welcomed if you express yourself clearly and directly in the simplest language. Plain, simple words are more easily understood. A properly paragraphed message is required for the purpose of clarity.

 **Task 2**

Try to avoid ambiguous expressions. Compare the following expressions to see which is better.

1. As to the steamers sailing from Hong Kong to San Francisco, we have bimonthly direct services.
2. We have two direct sailings every month from Hong Kong to San Francisco.
3. We have a direct sailing every two months from Hong Kong to San Francisco.

Task 3

Please translate the Chinese into English in a SIMPLE and CONCRETE way.

1. 这份合同要求 10 月 10 日之前签名。

2. 非常感谢您 3 万美金的支票。

3. 抱歉我很难赞同。

Sample 3 Replying complaints

Dear Mr. Clinton,

Thank you for your letter of 12 May 2013 concerning faulty goods purchased in our store in London.

I am very sorry indeed that you were not satisfied with the pencils that you bought from our store.

Our company is always trying to improve the quality of its merchandise and we are very unhappy when one of our products does not give satisfaction. In fact, this was due to the breakdown of our packing machine.

In the meantime I regret the disappointment you were caused. As a gesture of goodwill, I have pleasure in refunding the cost of the pencils. And enclose a gift voucher that you can use in our London branch.

Thank you for bringing this matter to our attention. I hope any further purchases you may make at our stores will be up to our usual high standards.

Yours sincerely,

Paul Harvey

Customer Relations

Writing Tips

We should bear in mind the point that business letters play an important role in the development of goodwill and friendly trade relationships. Therefore, correctness and courtesy are the key guides in writing business letter.

Correctness means not only proper expressions with correct grammar, punctuation and spelling, but also appropriate tone, which is a help to achieve the purpose. Business letters must be factual information accurate figures and exact terms in particular, for they involve the right, the duties and the interest of both sides often as the base of all kinds of documents.

Courtesy means to show tactfully in your letters the honest friendship, thoughtful appreciation, sincere politeness, considerate understanding and heartfelt respect. Compare the following examples.

🐧 *Task 4*

Try to compare which expression is more POLITE.

1. We have received your letter of 20 May, and we are sending you our latest catalogue.
2. We have received with many thanks your letter of 20 May, and we take the pleasure of sending you our latest catalogue.

🐧 *Task 5*

Please fill in the blank to complete the sentences in an appropriate way.

1. We _____(感谢)your letter of 14 June 2013 concerning the faulty goods purchased in our store.
2. Kindly be _____(通知)that the pencils you bought are not satisfactory.
3. We'll be _____(感激)for the complete to send related materials to our office prior to our meeting.

🔵 *Part III   Vocabulary in Use*

book /buk/	v.	arrange for and reserve 预订
concerning /kən'sə:niŋ/	prep.	have to do with or be relevant to 关于，就……而论
budget /'bʌdʒit/	n.	a sum of money allocated for a particular purpose 预算
campaign /kæm'pein/	n.	a series of actions advancing a principle or tending toward a particular end 运动；活动
grateful /'greitfl/	adj.	a feeling or show gratitude 感激的
discount /'diskaunt/	n.	the act of reducing the selling price of merchandise 折扣
issue /'iʃu:/	n.	an important question that is in dispute and must be settled 重要问题，争论的问题
inconvenience /ˌinkən'vi:niəns/	n.	a difficulty that causes anxiety or discomfort 不方便，麻烦
purchase /'pɜ:tʃəs/	v.	obtain by purchase; acquire by means of a financial transaction 购买，采购；换得
merchandise /'mɜ:tʃəndais/	n.	commodities offered for sale 商品
breakdown /'breikdaun/	n.	the act of disrupting an established order so it fails to continue 崩溃，倒塌，故障

regret /rɪ'ɡret/	*v.*	feel sad about the loss or absence of 后悔，遗憾
refund /'ri:fʌnd/	*v.*	pay back 退还；归还或偿还
enclose /ɪn'kləʊz/	*v.*	enclose or enfold completely with or as if with a covering 把……装入信封；附上
voucher /'vaʊtʃə/	*n.*	a printed pieced of paper that can be used instead of money to pay for sth. 代金券
concreteness /'kɒnkri:tnɪs/	*n.*	the quality of being concrete (not abstract) 具体性
courtesy /'kɜ:təsɪ/	*n.*	a courteous or respectful or considerate act 礼貌，谦恭

Expressions

1. I am writing to inform you that... 写信通知您……

   I am writing to enquire about... 写信咨询……

   I am writing apologize for... 写信道歉……

   I am writing to complain about... 写信投诉……

2. advertising campaign 广告宣传活动

3. instead of 而不是

4. in addition (to) 此外

5. rather than 而不是

6. considering 考虑到

7. look forward to... 期待……

8. due to 由于……

   owing to…

   because of…

   thanks to…

9. as a gesture of goodwill 作为一种友善的姿态

10. bring sth. to one's attention 使某人注意

    call one's attention 提醒某人注意

    draw one's attention 引起某人注意

    pay attention to…注意

11. be up to…达到（数量、程度等）；至多有；能胜任

⭐ Part IV   Practical Writing Tasks

Practice 1 Terms
Match the following business English terms and phrases with their proper Chinese meaning.

1. Business letters of inquiries   A. 商务索赔函

2. Business letters of complaints   B. 商务提案

3. Business letters of offers   C. 商务询盘函

4. Business letters of claims   D. 合同有效性

5. Business letters of counter-offers   E. 后续询问信函

6. Follow-up letter   F. 商务投诉函

7. Business memo   G. 商务报盘函

8. Business proposal   H. 商务还盘函

9. Validity of contracts   I. 结尾敬语

10. Complimentary close   J. 商务备忘录

Practice 2 Fill in the blanks with the words and expressions given bellow. Change the form where necessary.

inform	sample	available	concern	plan
regret	help	enclose	attractive	reception

1. Thank you for your enquiry of 5 May _____ silk blouses.

2. We _____ to say that we do not manufacture clothing to your own designs to the highest European standards.

3. We hope that this will be of _____ to you and wish you every success in your business dealings.

4. I _____ an illustrated supplement tour catalogue.

5. It covers the latest designs, which are now _____ from stock.

6. We believe that you will find our new designs most _____.

7. They should get a very good _____ in your market.

8. We would be very happy to send _____ to you for closer inspection.

9. For your information, we are _____ a range of classical English dinner services.

10. We will keep you _____ on our progress and look forward to hearing from you.

Practice 3 Translation

I. Translate the following sentences from Chinese into English.

1. 从您的来信得知，已发现5把椅子在装运过程中受到损坏。

2. 我们希望本月底以前收到您应付的金额。

3. 我们希望你们能对货物满意，并期待收到你们更多的订单。

4. 对于任何不便之处我们再次表示歉意。

5. 请告知您能给我们什么样的优惠。

II. Translate the following sentences from English into Chinese.

1. We would appreciate it if you could send some samples of the material so that we can examine the texture and the quality.

2. We've compared your price with those from the other suppliers and your price is almost 5% higher than that from the American and German suppliers.

3. Please confirm that you'll execute our order by the end of November so that we can be ready for the selling season.

4. I'm sorry that the goods you inquired for are not available, since they are out of stock now.

5. Would you please handle all the shipping formalities and insurance, and send us copies of the bill of lading, the commercial invoice, and their insurance certificate?

Practice 4 Practical Writing
Write a letter, using the following information.

> ※ Suppose you are intending to buy large quantities of digital cameras. Before you place an order, you'd like to see some samples and know something about price, earliest delivery date and terms of payment.
>
> ※ You are required to write a letter of enquiry of 120 words according to the given situation.

_____

_____

_____

_____

_____

_____

Part V Key Sentences for Reference

※ Since we are on the point of concluding an important business with the captioned company, we would like to know its financial standing and modes of business.

我们即将与上述公司达成一项重要贸易，请告诉我们有关该公司的资信及经营状况。

※ We would appreciate it very much if you could send us your catalog together with the current sales terms.

如能寄来商品目录以及现行销售条款，我们将不胜感激。

※ Would you please tell us frankly whether you think it advisable to give the captioned company a credit to the extent of $30,000?

请直言相告，我们给该公司 $30,000 的信用额度可行吗？

※ We would appreciate your paying the bill without delay.

请从速结账。

※ Specializing in the export of household appliance, we wish to express our desire to cooperate with you in this line.

我们专门从事家用电器的出口业务，所以我们期望与贵公司在这一领域的合作。

※ It would be very much appreciated if you would confirm the shipping arrangement as soon as possible.

请尽快确认装运安排。

※ We should be pleased to receive your illustrated catalogue and price list of plastic kitchenware.

请寄给我们你方图示的产品目录和塑料餐具价目表。

※ We are grateful to you for having offered us the information about your local markets.

感谢你们向我们提供当地市场情况。

※ Would you please mail us some sample materials from which the items are made?

请给我们寄一些制造这些产品的样料。

※ We should like to know if you are prepared to grant us a special discount.

请问你们能否给我们特殊的折扣？

※ We shall be obliged if you will send us some samples with the best terms at your earliest convenience.

如果贵公司能及早寄给我们一些样品并且给予最优惠的条件，我们将不胜感激。

※ We would like to have a booklet which includes your latest designs for building up the equipment.

我们想要一本含有建造该设备所用的最新设计图样的小册子。

※ I am writing about possibility of establishing a long-term business relationship since both of us fall into the scope of electronic industry.

鉴于我们双方都从事电子工业方面的业务，现特致函探讨是否有建立长期业务关系的可能。

Business Memos

Learning Objectives

To be proficient in

➢ understanding useful words and expressions often used in memos;

➢ mastering the essential elements included in a business memo;

➢ practicing writing business memos.

Part I Warming-up Activities

Task 1

Read the following passage to learn about business memo.

Memo is a simple and efficient message that is used to remind of or draw someone's attention to certain matters. It is efficient because its format conveys the writer's ideas quickly and directly to the readers.

First of all, business memos are used to solve problem and keep "memory". They solve problems either by informing the reader about new information, like policy changes, price increases, etc., or by persuading the reader to take an action, such as attending a meeting, using less paper, or changing a current production procedure. Regardless of the specific goal, memos are most effective when they connect the purpose of the writer with the interests and needs of the reader.

Another purpose of memos is to be filed up as part of an organization's "memory". Memos are often the first documents gathered in legal cases and policy disputes with organizations. Even though the primary audience, purpose, and your role in writing a memo might well defined, keep in mind the broader implications of the memo as a document representing you, relationships within an organization, and the organization itself.

Unlike business letters, which include inside addresses, salutations, and complimentary closings, business memos have just two sections: the heading and the body. To simplify the communication process, many firms and organizations use memo pads with pre-designed formats. You just file the relative words in the blank space, and then a memo will be produced in a few minutes.

To begin with, the **heading** has four parts: TO, FROM, DATE and SUBJECT. They can be placed in vertical or horizontal order.

In addition, the **body** can be divided into four sections: **opening segment, summary segment, discussion segment** and **close segments** in formal and complicated memos.

1) The purpose of a memo is usually found in the opening paragraph and is presented in three parts: The context and problem, the specific assignment or task, and the purpose of the memo. 2) If your memo is longer than a page, you may want to include a separate summary segment. This segment provides a brief statement of the key recommendations you have reached. These will help your reader understand the key points of the memo immediately. This segment may also include references to methods and sources you have used in your research, but remember to keep it brief. 3) The discussion segments are the parts in which you get to include all the details that support your ideas. 4) After the reader has absorbed all of your information, you want to close with a courteous ending that states what action you want your reader to take.

Task 2

Work in pairs and write down the key elements involved in a business memo.

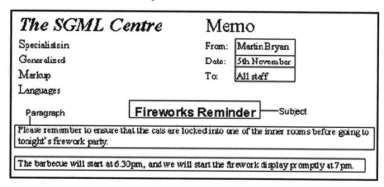

_____

_____

_____

Task 3

Work in pairs to discuss the following questions.

1. What is business memo? Is it like common business letter?

2. What is the purpose of business memo?

3. What is the layout of business memo?

4. What do you mean by opening segment?

5. What is the function of summary segment?

Part II   Sample Study &Writing Tips

Sample 1 Business Memo

To: All Users of the Email System

From:IT Department

Date: 12 August, 2013

Subject: Scheduled Email Server Maintenance

The main email server will be taken down for routine maintenance this Saturday from 11am to 2:30pm. This maintenance window will allow us to do a full system backup, database maintenance to increase speed and reliability, and do our monthly update.

The Email Server will not be available this Saturday from 11am to 2:30pm.

If you have any questions or a critical reason to reschedule this maintenance, please call the help desk directly at 010-88647856.

Thank you.

IT Department

Writing Tips

Whether business memo is formal or not, the part of **OPENING** should start directly and restate and amplify the main idea. In the part of **BODY**, try to explain and discuss the topic by using graphic highlighting to facilitate reading, comprehension, and retention. In the part of **CLOSING**, summarize the message, or provide a closing thought.

Conciseness is a very important principle to observe in business memo writing. As an efficient form of internal communication, memos contain only what you intend to convey. Often you do not have to provide background information when you are certain the reader knows about the subject discussed in the memo, nor do you need to make as much goodwill effort as you do in letters to your business partners outside of the organization.

Task 1

Compare the following expression to see which one is more appropriate in the part of OPENING:

1. This is to inform you that we must complete the annual operating budgets shortly. Over the past two months many supervisors have met to discuss their departmental needs.
2. All supervisors and coordinators will meet June 3 at 10 a.m. to work out the annual operating budgets for their departments.

Sample 2 Business memo

To: Everyone
From: John Doe
Date: 24 April, 2012
Subject: **SMOKING**

Due to several complaints, smoking will no longer be allowed near the main doorway into the building. If you choose to smoke before or after work, you may continue to do so in the alley by the dumpsters. This policy change is in effect for everyone that works for XYZ, Inc. with NO exceptions.

Failure to comply with this policy will result in a one-timeWARNING before a written reprimand will be applied to your permanent file and your annual review will be affected.

If you have any questions related to this policy, please contact the Director of HR at 010-89346599 or via email at joan@xyx.com. This is the only notice that will be sent on this issue and it will be displayed in the lunchroom and by the main door into the building.

Thank you.
John Doe

Writing Tips

Persuasion and visual signaling are well tactfully written in the above business memo.

➤*Persuasion* means business memo should be full, strong and reasonable to persuade person to take the relative action willingly. Hence, try to be cordial, straightforward, avoiding chitchat, but striving toward a relaxed, persuasive and conversational style.

➤*Visual signaling*

i.Effective memo writers highlight important words, phrases, points, and sections with

ii. numbers or bullets listed vertically;

iii. **boldface** or *italics*;

iv. headings and subheadings.

Task 2

Complete the sentences with the words given in the blank.

attention	prohibit	employee
memo	intra	apply

1) _____ all staff: effective immediately, all office communication is restricted to email correspondence as official 2) _____ . The use of instance message program by employee during work hour is strictly 3) _____ . Does this apply to 4) _____ office communication only or relate also restrict external communications? It should 5) _____ to all communications. Not only in this office between 6) _____ , but also any outside communications.

Sample 3 Business Memo

To: Ms. Iris Anderson, Trust Officer

From: Sam Jones, Payroll Accounting

Date: 23 October 2009

Subject: Request for Update on Stock Option Participation

We need an update on those employees in your department who are participating in the company stock option plan.

Please list the names of those who are currently participating and their years of service. Also list anyone who will be eligible for participation next year.

Be sure to turn in this information to me by 28 October.

Thank you.

Sam Jones

Writing Tips

Business memo should be written by the principle of *clearness*. That is to say, memos are written to get someone to do or understand something—be it to spend money, meet a deadline, constructively criticize, or say yes or no. When you do so, people who read memos, cannot hesitate to take action to observe the instruction of memos.

🐧 *Task 3*

Please try to complete the business memo with the given Chinese.

To:Katherine Chu, Regional Manager

From:Stephen Yu, Sales

Date:16 August 2005

Subject:My resignation

I have appreciated very much my four years working for the company. The training has been excellent and I have 1) _____ (获得宝贵的经验)working within an efficient and professional team environment. 2) _____ (尤其是)I have appreciated your personal guidance during the first year of my career. I feel now that 3) _____ (是时候进一步开发)my knowledge and skills base in a different environment. I would like to leave, if possible, in a month's time on Saturday, 17 September. This will allow me to complete my current workload. I hope that this suggested arrangement is 4) _____ (对公司是可以接受的).

Once again, 5) _____ (感谢您的支持).

Stephen Yu

🔵 *Part III   Vocabulary in Use*

server /'sɜːvə/	*n.*	a computer that provides client stations with access to files and printers as shared resources to a computer network 计算机服务器
maintenance /'meɪntənəns/	*n.*	activity involved in maintaining something in good working order 维修，保养
database /'deɪtəbeɪs/	*n.*	an organized body of related information 数据库，信息库
reliability /rɪˌlaɪə'bɪlətɪ/	*n.*	the trait of being dependable or reliable 可靠，可信赖
critical /'krɪtɪkl/	*adj.*	urgently needed; absolutely necessary; vital 决定性的，关键的
alley /'ælɪ/	*n.*	a narrow street with walls on both sides 胡同，小巷
dumpster /'dʌmpstə/	*n.*	a container designed to receive and transport and dump waste 装垃圾的铁桶
exception /ɪk'sepʃn/	*n.*	an instance that does not conform to a rule or generalization 例外，除外
reprimand /'reprɪmɑːnd/	*n.*	an act or expression of criticism and censure 训斥，谴责

permanent/'pɜ:mənənt/	*adj.*	continuing or enduring without marked change in status or condition or place 永久性的，永恒的
via/'vaɪə/	*prep.*	by ways of; through 经由
accounting/ə'kaʊntɪŋ/	*n.*	the occupation of maintaining and auditing records and preparing financial reports for a business 会计
persuasion/pə'sweɪʒn/	*n.*	the act of persuading (or attempting to persuade); communication intended to induce belief or action 说服力，劝说
conciseness/kən'saɪsnɪs/	*n.*	terseness and economy in writing and speaking achieved by expressing a great deal in just a few words 简洁，简明
boldface/'bəʊldfeɪs/	*n.*	a typeface with thick heavy lines 黑体字，粗体铅字
chitchat /'tʃɪttʃæt/	*n.*	talk socially without exchanging too much information 闲聊，闲谈

Expressions

1. system backup 系统备份
2. in effect 有效；事实上
   take effect 生效
   to the effect 其大意是
3. comply with 服从，遵从；应；顺应；照办
   【联想】conform to…　　abide by…　　in accordance with…
4. result in 导致
   result from… 由……造成
5. annual review 年度审核，年度总结
6. be related to 与……相关
   be relevant to…
7. HR=Human Resources 人力资源
8. Trust Officer 信托官员
9. stock option 职工优先认股权，在指定时期内定价定额购股权
10. be eligible for 适合于，有……资格
    be qualified for…
11. be sure to do 一定能做
    be bound to do…
12. turn in 上交 (=hand in)
    turn down（婉言）拒绝；音量调低
    turn to sb. 转向某人（for help）
    turn up 把音量调大；出现（=show up）

Part IV   Practical Writing Tasks

Practice 1 Complete the information according to the sample.

The HR manager, John Smith, decides to hold a meeting regarding personnel training. The meeting will be held in Room 202 at 2p.m. on October 30th. He would like all department managers to attend the meeting. He wishes to write a business memo on October 28th in order to inform them of it.

Memorandum

Receiver: _____

Sender: _____

Date: _____

Subject: _____

A meeting on personnel training will be held in _____ at 2p.m. on October 30th.

John Smith

Practice 2 Fill in the blanks with the words and expressions given bellow. Change the form where necessary.

appreciate	free	reference	benefit	adopt
remind	response	board	cost	propose

1. I would like to _____ you that our office is in want of a new English typewriter.

2. This is further to your memo dated June 6, 2006, in which you proposed that employees _____ the "punch in" system.

3. The _____ of directors approved your proposal at the meeting last week.

4. I believe these changes will decrease the product _____ .

5. Please let me know your _____ to these suggestions.

6. Please feel _____ to contact me if you need further information.

7. I highly _____ your considerations to these proposals.

8. The purpose of this memo is to recommend a new shelving system for books in the _____ section of our library.

9. I _____ that we switch to an open-shelf system at once.

10. The _____ open shelves would be a reduction in personnel and free access to a needed library resource.

Practice 3 Translation

I. Translate the following sentences from Chinese into English.

1.请注意，健康与安全检查专员明天将来我处检查工作。

2. 公司认为有必要削减费用。

3. 若有人想在春节顺带休年假，请提前通知各自的经理。

4. 凡骑车上班的员工请将自行车存放在办公楼后面。

5. 我已接到会议通知，在此申请一部投影仪于会上使用。

II. Translate the following sentences from English into Chinese.

1. Both parties acknowledge that they do not acquire any right in or any intellectual property rights (including without limitation, copyright, trademark, trade secret, know-how) of the other Party under this MOU.

2. Neither Party shall make any announcement or disclosure concerning the MOU (Memorandum of Understanding) without the other Party's prior written consent except as may be reasonably required by law.

3. The terms and conditions of this MOU shall be amended only by mutual written consent between the Parties.

4. China and the United States on Wednesday signed MOU regarding cooperation in antitrust and antimonopoly investigations.

5. I would appreciate the form filled in and returned to the General Office by April 10, 2009.

Practice 4 Practical Writing
Write a memo, using the following information.

Memo for the Month of English Program

※送：各位校领导

※自：校学生会

※日期：2008/05/20

※主题：关于开展英语活动月的计划书

※内容：

　校学生会拟开展英语主题活动月，时间：2008 年 6 月；

　主要活动介绍，包括英语朗读、演讲、辩论、歌曲比赛及英语话剧等，请领导予以支持。

Part V Key Sentences for Reference

※ All the activities of both parties shall comply with the memorandum.

双方的一切活动都应遵守备忘录规定。

※ Both parties agree to change the time of shipment to August and change US dollar into Renminbi.

交货期改为 8 月并将美元折合成人民币。

※ Your early reply is highly appreciated.

承蒙早日回复，不胜感激。

※ Please kindly send us your price list and catalogue.

恳请寄给我方贵方价格单和产品目录。

※ We should be obliged for your immediate amendment of the L/C to enable us to make timely shipment.

敬请立刻修改信用证以便我方及时发货。

※ Party B is hereby appointed by Party A as its exclusive sales agent in London.

甲方委托乙方为在伦敦的独家销售代理。

※ This MOU is made out in four copies, two for either party.

本谅解备忘录一式四份，双方各执两份为凭。

※ This MOU is signed and interpreted pursuant to the laws of the People's Republic of China.

本谅解备忘录是根据中华人民共和国法律签订并依其解释。

※ Would you kindly quote us your lowest price FOB London ASAP?

烦请贵方尽快报伦敦离岸最低价。

※ We confirm having cabled you a firm offer subject to your reply reaching us by October 10th.

现确认已向贵方电发实盘，10 月 10 日前复到有效。

※ The message we want to get across to the customer is that his or her satisfaction is our first priority.

我们想传达给顾客的信息是，他们的满意是我们的第一宗旨。

※ By lowering our prices we hope to increase sales volume and capture a larger share of the market.

通过降低价格，我们希望能增加销售量，进而扩大市场占有率。

※ In reply to your enquiry of June 7, 1990, I respectfully offer my latest quotation herewith.

兹回复贵方 1990 年 6 月 7 日来函，特随函奉上我方最新报价。

Business Notice & Poster

Learning Objectives

To be proficient in

➢ understanding the useful words and expressions used in business notice and poster;

➢ writing notices and posters;

➢ dealing with unnecessary words correctly.

⊛ *Part I Warming-up Activities*

🐧 *Task 1*

Read the following passage about notice and poster in practical business writings.

Notice and poster are both practical business writings.

Notice is a written or printed statement that gives information or directions to the general public. As one of the most commonly used practical writings, notice is used to provide the public with various kinds of information, ranging from lectures, meetings, conference, trips, and the Lost Found to sports events, films, and parties.

There are many types of business notice, say, notice of business opening, notice of a newly-established branch, notice of announcing amalgamation, notice of the move of a company, notice of announcing the appointment of sole agent, notice of improving welfare, meeting notice, notice of appointment, and notice of employment offer.

Generally the body of a notice should contain the following contents: time, place, sponsor and other details. The notices should be written briefly, appropriately and promptly. The date and the signature of the person or the organization that writes the notice can be omitted; the organization that writes the notice and the person or organization noticed should be in the third person, but if there is a salutation in front of the body, the person or organization noticed should be in the second person.

An effective notice or announcement usually follows the principles stated below:

1. State the matter in the first line of the letter body or in the first paragraph of the letter.

2. Specify the background, details, explanations or qualifications.

3. If the event intends to motivate actions, you can provide this information in the last paragraph.

In general, a poster consists of the name of activity, participants, time, place, sponsor and signature. Posters have no fixed layouts. Their styles are various. But their words should be concise, clear and complete.

🐧 *Task 2*

Work in pairs and read the following conversation to learn about business notice writing.

Neil: Hi, Stella, you have been in this company for several years. Could you tell me how to write a business notice?

Stella: Sure. First of all, the notice should observe the following five principles: where, when, who, what and how. For example, *The next Monthly Management Meeting will be held at 10:00 a.m. on Monday, April 5, at Meeting Room A.*

Neil: I see, but if there is a change in the schedule of the meeting how to write the notice?

Stella: You can follow the format of writing like *The next Monthly Management Meeting (previously scheduled on Monday next week) has been rescheduled on Friday, April 9, same time, same place.*

Neil: Great! And what if I inform the specific arrangements of the meeting ahead of time in the notice?

Stella: You can start from a second line with the detailed agenda in the notice.

Neil: And how to close the notice?

Stella: Since you have informed the agenda of the meeting in advance, you can say *If there are any other items you would like to be placed on the agenda, let me know by e-mail by the end of this week. Thank you.*

Neil: Thank you very much. You are very helpful.

Stella: Not at all.

🐧 Task 3

Work in pairs to discuss the following questions.

1. What's the function of business notice?

2. How many types of business notice are there?

3. How many elements are involved in business notice writing?

4. How can you write an effective notice?

5. Is there any fixed layout in business poster?

⚝ Part II   Sample Study &Writing Tips

Sample 1 Poster

Friendly Basketball Match

All Are Warmly Welcome

Teams: Agricultural University vs Normal University

Time: 8:30 a.m., Nov. 24, 2001(Saturday)

Place:Provincial Gymnasium

Sponsor:The Physical Cultural Academy

Please contact the Physical Culture Academy for tickets (limited to 100). Basketball fans should hurry. Three college buses will take fans to the match. Fans are expected to gather at the college gate at 8:00 a.m. sharp the day of the game.

Writing Tips

Good business poster should be easier to read and easier to comprehend. Clarity is always a goal when writing business poster. To get this, you should keep in mind the purpose of your poster is ambiguous will cause trouble to both sides. Hence clear and familiar words are better used in writing. On one hand you'll stand tall in your reader's eyes if you replace long words with shorter ones. On the other hand, avoiding words with different meanings, which may create ambiguous meanings.

 **Task 1**

Please complete the following poster with the given information.

> **Friendly Basketball Match**
> **All Are Welcome**
>
> 1) _____ (学生会组织) of our school; a friendly 2) _____ (篮球比赛) will be held between the overseas students and 3) _____ (研究生) on the campus 4) _____ (篮球场) at 4 p.m. on Saturday, June 10, 2012.
>
> The Student Union
> Thursday, June 8

Sample 2 Notice

> Feb.25, 2006
>
> Dear Sir/Madam,
>
> Thanks to the large increase in the volume of our trade with this country we have decided to open a branch here, with Mr. Wang as manager. The new branch will open on the 1st of March and from that date all orders and inquiries should be sent to Mr. Wang at the above address instead of our London office.
>
> We take this opportunity to express our thanks for your cooperation in the past.
>
> We hope the new arrangements will lead to even better results.
>
> Yours,
> Wen Fang

Writing Tips

You should state your purpose at the beginning of your notice. The question "what is your point" is very common with audiences. In general, people prefer to get a preview of the main idea so that they know what to expect. Time is an important factor for business people because they do not have much of it. So it is important to state your purpose or "the bottom line" for writing at the beginning of your document.

 **Task 2**

Here is an example of requesting employment verification. What do you think of the following writing? Does the writer reveal his or her purpose at the beginning of writing?

Example 1

Dear General Director:

On June 24, I received a phone call from Mrs. King in New York, who was once a data entry clerk in your Ohio office. She was under the direct supervision of ...

Example 2

Dear General Director:

Would you verify the employment of Mrs. King? She was a data entry clerk in your Ohio office (fill in the details)

Sincerely.

Sample 3 Notice

Notice

Notice is hereby given that the annual general meeting of the shareholders of our company will be held at the Bankers' Club on June 1.

February13th, 2012

Writing Tips

You must have a clear idea of what you wish to convey to the readers in notice writing. When you are sure about what to say, say it in plain, simple words. Good, straightforward, and simple English is what is needed for business notice.

➤*Keeping Your Sentences Simple*

Try to write the sentences that are much easier to understand and get straight to the point, otherwise, there may bring up room for misunderstanding with that statement.

➤*Keeping Related Words Together*

The position of the words in a sentence is the principal means of showing their relationship. The writer must therefore, so far as possible, bring together the words, and groups of words, which are related in thought, and keep apart those which are not so related.

Task 3

Please write an English notice with the given information.

通知

江苏大学游泳池将与今年 6 月 15 日对外开放。开放时间早 8:00 至晚 10:00；费用成人一小时 3 元，儿童 2 元。自备泳衣。

校长办公室

2012 年 6 月 12 日

_____

_____

_____

_____

_____

_____

_____

_____

✦ *Part III   Vocabulary in Use*

agricultural /ˌægrɪ'kʌltʃərəl/	*adj.*	of agriculture 农业的
normal /'nɔ:ml/	*adj.*	usual and ordinary 规范的
provincial /prə'vɪnʃl/	*adj.*	connected with the parts of a country outside the capital 省的
gymnasium /dʒɪm'neɪzɪəm/	*n.*	a room containing exercise equipment 体操房，体育馆
academy /ə'kædəmɪ/	*n.*	an institution for the advancement of art or science or literature 学院，学会
volume /'vɒljuːm/	*n.*	the total amount of sth 量
branch /brɑːntʃ/	*n.*	an administrative division of some larger or more complex organization 分支，部门
order /'ɔːdə(r)/	*n.*	a commercial document used to request someone to supply something in return for payment and providing specifications and quantities 订购
inquiry /ɪn'kwaɪərɪ/	*n.*	an instance of questioning 询问
arrangement /ə'reɪndʒmənt/	*n.*	the thing arranged or agreed to 安排，筹划
hereby /hɪə'baɪ/	*adv.*	by this statement 兹，借此
shareholder /'ʃeəhəʊldə/	*n.*	someone who owns shares in a business 股东

Expressions

1. The Physical Cultural Academy 体育文化研究会
2. be limited to... 限于……
3. 8:00 sharp 8 点整
4. owing to... 由于……
   due to…
   thanks to…
   because of…
5. decide to do... 决定做……
6. take this opportunity to do something 借此机会做某事

7. the annual general meeting 年会

8. express one's thanks for... 表达感谢

9. lead to 带来，导致

result in…

contribute to…

attribute…to…

Part IV   Practical Writing Tasks

Practice 1 Complete the notice with the following expressions.

a number of activities	ranked	are welcome
are preparing to	with the efforts of	

Notice

We 1) _____ celebrate the 15th anniversary of our company. 2) _____ all our staff, our company is now 3) _____ as one of the leading companies in the field of computer science in our country. To thank and encourage all the employees, we will hold 4) _____ . The employees' suggestions and proposals 5) _____ and those being accepted will be awarded. Please hand in your proposals to our office or e-mail them to cso@126.com .

If you still have any questions, please telephone the office at 0742-8797528.

Company Office

July 26,2013

Practice 2 Fill in the blank with the words and expressions given bellow. Change the form where necessary.

branch	express	lead to	advantage	confidence
guarantee	owing to	order	behalf	notify

1. _____ the large increase in the volume of our trade with this country we have decided to open a branch here, with Mr. Wang Lo as manager.

2. The new _____ will open on 1st March.

3. From that date all _____ and inquiries should be sent to Mr. Wang Lo at the above address, instead of to our London office.

4. We take this opportunity to _____ our thanks for your cooperation in the past.

5. We hope the new arrangements will _____ even better results.

6. We wish to _____ you that Mr. Robert Smart, who has been our representative in Southwest

England.

7. For the past seven years has left our service and therefore no longer has authority to take orders or collect accounts on our _____ .

8. We would be pleased if you would take full _____ of our services and favorable shopping conditions.

9. We fully _____ the quality of our products.

10. We appreciate the _____ you have placed in us in the past and look forward to continued dealings with you.

Practice 3 Translation

I. Translate the following sentences from Chinese into English.

1.本厂已迁移到上述地址，特此通知。

2.我方已在本市开店，特此通知。

3.本店于 5 月 1 日改为股份有限公司。

4.通过这些渠道，他们会发来很多订单，特此函告。

5.凭票入场。

II. Translate the following sentences from English into Chinese.

1. We acquaint you that we have established ourselves as general agents under the title of Microsoft. Co.

2. We are pleased to inform you that our business will be turned into a private corporation on the 1st of August.

3. We inform you that on the 21st of this month, we established in this city a dry-goods business under the firm-name of Kate King.

4. Having established ourselves in this city, as merchants and general agents, we take the liberty of acquainting you of it, and solicit the preference of your order.

5. I have now to inform you that I shall in future carry on the business under the style of Stone. Co.

Practice 4 Practical Writing

Write a poster, using the following information.

※ 不能错过的机会！

※ 精彩、激烈的国际足球比赛赛讯

※ 中国队　对　澳大利亚队

※ 地点：首都体育馆

※ 时间：2008 年 6 月 28 日下午 3 点半

※ 请到接待处购票，欢迎前往助兴！

Part V   Key Sentences for Reference

※ To mark this special occasion, customers will be offered with a special opening discount.

为庆祝这个特殊的日子，所有顾客将享受开业打折优惠。

※ They delayed the effective date from June 6 to July 27.

他们将生效日期从 6 月 6 日推迟到了 7 月 27 日。

※ We are happy to inform you that owing to steady growth of our firm in the past years and in view of facilitating business expansion, we have decided to move our office to …

我们很高兴地通知您，鉴于我公司业务的稳定增长以及为了更好地拓展业务，我们已决定将公司迁至……

※ A welcoming ceremony for our new CFO, Mr. Wooden, will be held in California Grand Hotel, Room 4088, at 6 p.m. on Saturday, May 26th.

欢迎我们的新任财务总监伍顿先生的典礼将于 5 月 26 日，星期六晚上 6 点，在加利福尼亚大酒店 4088 房间举行。

※ Mr. Dean has replaced Ms. Larson as the Oceanside sales manager.

Mr. Dean 已取代 Ms. Larson 成为滨海区业务经理。

※ Ms. Harris will be taking over for Mr. Pierce on accounts payable.

Ms. Harris 将接管 Mr. Pierce 负责的应付账款事宜（accounts payable）。

※ Mr. Evans has been designated Director of Operations.

Mr. Evans 已被派任为营运总监（Director of Operations）。

※ If you have any questions regarding these changes, please feel free to contact us.

如果您对这些变动有任何问题，请尽快和我们联络。

※ Owing to an exceptionally busy season the goods your ordered had to be shipped behind schedule.

由于本季度格外繁忙，你方订货被迫推迟发运。

※ One of our repair centers has been newly opened in your city. Will you kindly contact them for the service? The charge is for our account.

我方在你方城市新设一个修理点，请您和他们联系维修服务，费用由我方负责。

※ We advise you with pleasure that we have this day sent by the Northwest Railway to your final address, freight paid, the captioned goods.

现高兴地通知你们，上述标题货物已于今日由西北铁路公司运往贵公司，运费已付。

※ Passengers are requested to note that the new timetable will come into effect on and from October 1, 2011.

旅客们请注意，新的列车时刻表将从 2011 年 10 月 1 日起实行。

※ This swimming pool will be open to public from July 12.Open hour: 2:00-6:00 pm (Mon.- Sat.) 1:00-7:00 pm (Sun.).

本游泳池将于 7 月 12 日起对外营业，开放时间是星期一至星期六：下午 2:00ˉ6:00；星期日：下午 1:00ˉ7:00。

※ The cinema will be closed from May 15 until further notice for repairs.

本院因内部装修，从 5 月 16 日起暂停营业，放映时间等待通知，特此通告。

Business Advertisement

Learning Objectives

To be proficient in

➢ using words and expressions for business advertisement;
➢ learning to use rhetorical devices in business advertisement;
➢ writing a business advertisement.

⭐ Part I Warming-up Activities

🐧 Task 1

Match the appropriate business advertisements.

1. Start ahead.

2. Time is what you make of it.

3. Fresh-up with Seven-up.

4. Engineered to move the human spirit.

🐧 Task 2

Read the following passage about advertisements and sum up the ways an advertisement is composed of.

The world is filled with advertisements. Different media are used in advertising. For example, radio commercials get millions of teenagers to shop for products made exclusively for them. Magazine ads showing models dressed in the latest style persuade women and men to buy new clothes in order to remain fashionable.

Each advertising medium serves a different purpose. However, critics of advertising argue that much advertising is merely persuasive and does not add to consumer's knowledge of the market. Moreover, exaggerated claims can mislead the consumer.

So what is advertisement? Advertisement is the non-personal communication of information usually paid for and usually persuasive in nature about products, services or ideas by identified sponsors through the various media.

Business advertisement is composed of headline, lead-in paragraph, body, signature and slogan.

The phrase or sentence in **Headline** should capture the readers' attention, arouse their interest, and entice them to read the rest of the ad.

Lead-in paragraph means not a mere shifting from headline to body; it is a summing-up of the whole writing. Readers can catch the main idea of the advertisement at reading the paragraph.

Body serves as the *main part of advertising information.*

➤ Be personal and friendly.

➤ Be simple and direct.

➤ Appeal to the senses.

➤ Answer questions about the product using facts.

➤ Add desire and urgency to the ad.

➤ Provide a personal call to action now or in the near future.

Signature or logo serves as *distinctive identification symbol for a business.*

Slogan is designed to be *explicit, refined, inflammatory* (煽动性的). A slogan is a *catchy phrase or words that identify a product or company.* Some advertisements also include the company's slogan, which is often presented with or near the signature.

 **Task 3**

Answer the following questions.

1. What is advertisement?

2. What is composed of business advertisement?

3. When kind of headline is eye-catching? Please take an example.

4. What is necessary in writing the body of business advertisement?

5. Which element is peculiar to business advertisement?

Part II Sample Study &Writing Tips

 # Sample 1 Job Advertisement

Lingua Franca

Marketing and sales associate

Lingua Franca is a leading developer of multimedia language training packages focusing on English for Spanish speakers and Spanish for English speakers. Our dynamic approach to language training was first marketed in 1996, and is now being used by teachers in twelve states. We are planning our international market penetration focusing on five Latin American countries. We are looking for a recent college graduate with a background in International Marketing and knowledge of Latin American business cultures to join our team.

We can offer you:

Training

Exciting challenges

Travel and possible relocation to a Latin American country

Competitive salary and bonus based on performance

Growth and promotion in a rapidly developing company with a market leading concept

We are looking for a college graduate with:

Degree in Business Administration and /or Marketing

Dynamic and outgoing personality

Knowledge of both written and spoken Spanish

If you would like to be part of a team whose goal is to become the market leader in multimedia language solutions, please contact our Head of Human Resources, Janet Avila, at Lingua Franca, 2050 Colorado Blvd. Pasadena, CA 93015 or e-mail <javila@lingua>

Writing Tips

Generally speaking, the language of advertising, mainly of so-called loaded languages, must be a language of immediate impact and rapid persuasion. It must bring the advertised products into attention, stress their qualities in the most attractive way, clearly outline the reasons for buying them, and preferably leave a memorable echo of what has been said about the products ringing in the reader's mind.

To achieve this, the language of advertising must be short, concise, vivid, attractive, and persuasive, which are fully displayed in advertising English. Lexical features, syntactic features and rhetorical features are supposed to be given much attention to when writing business advertisement.

The wide use of advertising has created a special style of English—advertising English. Its unique features, simple language and immense attraction separate it from other kind of business writing.

Task 1

Compare which headline is more appropriate as slogan in business advertisement.

1. Life-size sound from
2. He's alert! He's alive!
3. Small size speakers
4. He's High Protein Strong!

Sample 2 Cosmetics advertisement

PETAL-DROPS: FOR THE GIRL WHO WANTS A PETAL-SOFT SKIN

With Petal-Drops moisturizing Bath-Essence you can give your skin a petal-fresh softness and fragrance that will last the whole day through.

Because Petal-Drops is a special blend of mild soapless oil, delicately perfumed herbal essences and the gentlest of toning agents—all combined with loving care to give that oh-so-good-to-be-alive feeling.

Relax. Petal-Drops your way to a smooth, silky skin.

Choose from two exciting fragrances: new Petal-Drops "coriander"-with its spiced hint of seductiveness, or the classic Petal-Drops "lavender".

Writing Tips

There are lots of compound words in advertisement mainly because the element of compound words could be any part of speech, and has few limits in grammar and word order.

The following are the main ways of word forming:

adj+noun: short-term goal, high-fashion knitwear

noun+adj: the farmhouse-fresh faste, brand-new

v-ing+adj: shining-clean

noun+v-ed: honey-coated sugar puffs, home-made

adj/adv+v-ed: warm-hearted, perfectly-testured cakes

noun+v-ing: a relief-giving liquid, record-breaking

adj+v-ing: innocent-looking, fresh-tasting milk

adv+v-ing: hard-working, the best-selling soft toilet tissue

noun+noun: economy-size shredded wheat, a state-of-the-art cell sorcer

adv+noun: up-to-the-minute sculling

In addition, some prefixes or suffixes like "super-", "ex-", "-er", "-est" …etc, are often used to stress the high quality of the product.

Task 2

Please complete the body of business advertisement with the given information.

The home of your dream 1) _____ (等候) you behind this door, whether your taste 2) _____ (be) a country 3) _____ (庄园)estate or penthouse in the sky, you will find the following pages filled with the world's most 4) _____ (优雅的)residences.

Sample 3 Renting Advertisement

Location: Bei Yuan Apartment is located at No. 682, Xiaohe District, Guiyang

Description:

➤ Unfurnished, new paint, laundry facilities;

➤ Gas, water, power, and parking available;

➤ 1-bedroom, 2-bedroom and 3-bedroom apartments for rent or co-rent, condos for rent, and townhouses for rent;

➤ price ranges from RMB 500 to RMB 3,000 per month.

For availability and more details about rental, please call us TOLL FREE 400-800-4000

Contact: Fei Yang, Rental Office

Phone: 0851-66668888

Writing Tips

More simple sentences and less complex sentences are preferred in business advertisement. It will get better effect to use simple sentences than compound sentences, because the readers will get bored on reading complex sentences. Another reason is to reduce the cost of advertising, and effectively stimulate the consumers.

More interrogative sentences and imperative sentences are also welcome. According to statistics, in every 30 sentences there is one interrogative sentence, because interrogative sentences are quick and effective to arouse readers' response. Besides, the imperative sentences have a meaning of claiming, calling and commanding, similarly the goal of advertising is to persuade and urge consumers to accept its product or service. Therefore, there are lots of imperative sentences in advertising.

Task 3

Please fill in the blanks with the given words in its appropriate form.

course	study	access
close	overlook	

Country house in London, 1) _____ golf 2) _____ . 3) _____ to Richmond Park, good schools. Easy 4) _____ to city. 5 bedrooms, 2 receptions, 2 bathrooms, 5) _____ , work/playroom.

Part III   Vocabulary in Use

multimedia /ˌmʌltiˈmiːdiə/	*adj.*	of transmission that combine media of communication (text and graphics and sound etc.) 多媒体的
dynamic /daɪˈnæmɪk /	*adj.*	(approving) (of a person)having a lot of energy and a strong personality 充满活力的；精力充沛的；个性强的
approach /əˈprəʊtʃ/	*n.*	ideas or actions intended to deal with a problem or situation 方式，方法
penetration /ˌpenɪˈtreɪʃn /	*n.*	the act of entering into or through something 渗透，穿透
relocation /ˌriːləʊˈkeɪʃn/	*n.*	the act of changing your residence or place of business 迁移，再定位
competitive /kəmˈpetətɪv/	*adj.*	involving competition or competitiveness 竞争性的
bonus /ˈbəʊnəs/	*n.*	an additional payment (or other remuneration) to employees as a means of increasing output 红利，奖金，额外津贴
promotion /prəˈməʊʃn/	*n.*	act of raising in rank or position 晋升

outgoing /'aʊtgəʊɪŋ/	*adj.*	at ease in talking to others; somewhat extroverted 对人友好的；外向的
moisturize /'mɔɪstʃəraɪz/	*v.*	make (more) humid 增加水分，湿润
fragrance /'freɪgrəns/	*n.*	a distinctive odor that is pleasant 芬芳，香气
herbal /'ɜ:bəl/	*adj.*	of or relating to herbs 草药的，草本的
coriander /ˌkɒri'ændə(r)/	*n.*	herb with aromatic leaves and seed resembling parsley 芫荽；香菜
lavender /læ'vændɜ:/	*n.*	plant with sweet-smelling pale purple flowers 薰衣草
seductiveness /sɪ'dʌktɪvnɪs/	*n.*	tending to entice into a desired action or state 诱惑
unfurnished /ʌn'fɜ:nɪʃt/	*adj.*	not equipped with what is needed especially furniture 无装修的
available /ə'veɪləbl/	*adj.*	obtainable or accessible and ready for use or service 可用的
rental /'rentl/	*n.*	property that is leased or rented out or let 租赁

Expressions

1. lingua franca 混合语（任何混合国际商业用的语言），通用语，交际语

2. training package 训练包，成套的训练、培训

3. focus on 集中精神在……

   concentrate/center on…

   be bent on…

4. a market leading concept 市场的超前经营理念

5. becombined with 与……衔接在一起

   be linked with/to…

   be connected to…

6. laundry facilities 洗衣设施

7. range from…to… 从……到……范围内（变动）

   range between… and…

8. TOLL FREE 免费电话

9. Condos apartment 各户有独立产权的公寓（大楼）（condo 的名词复数）

⊙ Part IV   *Practical Writing Tasks*

Practice1 Terms
Match the following business English terms and phrases with their proper Chinese meaning.

1. Advertising audience   A. 地区广告

2. Target audience   B. 企业广告

3. Geographic area   C. 地方广告

4. Medium / media   D. 电子广告

5. Consumer advertising　　　　　　　E. 广告的听众、观众或读者

6. Business advertising　　　　　　　F. 印刷广告

7. Local advertising　　　　　　　　G. 目标听众、目标观众、目标群体

8. National advertising　　　　　　　H. 全球广告

9. International advertising　　　　　　I. 消费者广告

10. Global advertising　　　　　　　J. 媒体、媒介

11. Print advertising　　　　　　　　K. 国际广告

12. Electronic advertising　　　　　　L. 全国广告

13. Out-of-home advertising　　　　　M. 广告公司

14. Commercial advertising　　　　　　N. 媒体组织

15. Advertising agency　　　　　　　O. 商业广告

16. Media organization　　　　　　　P. 户外广告

Practice 2 Fill in the blank with the words and expressions given bellow. Change the form where necessary.

| with reference to | in reply to | advertisement | personnel | position |
| apply for | fill | consider | write | hear from |

1. _____ your advertisement in "China Daily" of 10 May 2004, I would like apply for the post of sales manager.

2. I should like to apply for the position mentioned in your _____ in today's "City Daily".

3. _____ your advertisement in today's "Business Weekly" for a secretary, I offer myself for the post.

4. I would like to _____ the post of Marketing Manager as advertised in today's newspaper.

5. Your advertisement for a _____ Manager in the newspaper of 11 May 2004 has interested me.

6. I feel I can _____ that position.

7. In response to your advertisement in the "Sunday Journal" of 11 May 2004, I wish to submit my application for the _____ of Director of Quality Control.

8. I wish to be _____ for the position of Personnel Manager advertised in today's journal.

9. I am _____ in response to your recent advertisement in the "China Daily", which invited applications for the position of Sales Coordinator.

10. I look forward to _____ you soon.

Practice 3 Translation

I. Translate the following sentences from Chinese into English.

1. 广告模式千变万化，可以是很死板的，也可以是很有互动性的。

2. 广告可以是一种艺术，只是加上了广告信息。

3. 一些简短的视频广告可以非常有效果。

4. 最新的广告趋势是运用一些幽默的，有创造性的，带有一定催促性的方式来吸引潜在顾客，很直接地做广告宣传。

5. 脱离传统的广告模式，你的商店访问量会直线上升。

II. Translate the following sentences from English into Chinese.

1. When it comes to advertising, you have many choices to get your message out.

2. Using advertising as a part of your marketing mix for your retail business is an essential tool, but if not used strategically, it can cost your business a lot of time and money.

3. Understanding the differences between popular advertising vehicles can be a worthwhile investment.

4. Use broadcast commercials like radio and cable television ads for a more targeted communication reach.

5. The prices of these forms of advertising can be a little more reasonable depending on the season, however, you may need to add production costs to your budget.

Practice 4 Practical Writing

Write a sales brochure, using the following information.

The following table displays a new product of a home appliance company. Suppose you work in the marketing department, please write a sales brochure for this new product.

Picture	Model	Functions
	Model: EB-3190EG	Halogen grill Electronic operation with LED display 10 microwave power levels 90 minutes time setting Auto menu & auto defrost function Child lock Quick start key

_____

_____

_____

_____

⭐ *Part V Key Sentences for Reference*

※ Best choice and best discount.

最佳选择，最大优惠。

※ Buy any two together and save 10% off both products.

一次性买俩，每个优惠 10%。

※ Easy to use and great value too.

好用实惠，物美价廉。

※ Free delivery to your door.

免费送货上门。

※ Furniture sale now on.

家具现降价销售。

※ We can provide the complete hospitality service.

我们提供热情周到的服务。

※ Peace of mind from the minute you buy.

买着放心。

※ courteous service

服务周到

※ dependable performance

性能可靠

※ have a reliable reputation

信誉可靠

※ durable in use

经久耐用

※ economy and durability

经济耐用

※ elegant and graceful

典雅大方

※ popular both at home and abroad

驰名中外

※ excellent in quality

品质优良

※ quality and quantity assured

保证质量

※ prime time

黄金时段

※ heading , headline

广告标题

※ hitchhike

免费广告

※ In-and-out promotion

促销

※ incentive

刺激销售

※ institutional advertising

建立永久声誉的广告

※ logotype

品牌名，出版物名

※ out of stock

脱销（尤指零售商）

※ Just do it.

只管去做。（耐克运动鞋）

※ Ask for more.

渴望无限。（百事流行鞋）

※ The taste is great.

味道好极了。（雀巢咖啡）

※ Feel the new space.

感受新境界。（三星电子）

※ Intelligence everywhere.

智慧演绎，无处不在。（摩托罗拉手机）

※ The choice of a new generation.

新一代的选择。（百事可乐）

※ We integrate, you communicate.

我们集大成，您超越自我。（三菱电工）

※ Take TOSHIBA, take the world.

拥有东芝，拥有世界。（东芝电子）

※ Let's make things better.

让我们做得更好。（飞利浦电子）

Business Letters of Invitation and Thanks

Learning Objectives

To be proficient in

➤ using words and expressions for business letters of invitation and thanks;

➤ using rhetorical devices in business invitation and thanks;

➤ writing business letters of invitation and thanks.

Part I Warming-up Activities

Task 1

Work in pairs and match the appropriate expressions used in business letters of invitation and thanks.

1. Request the pleasure of …

2. The favor of a reply is requested.

3. May I have the honor of your company at dinner?

4. I hope you are not too busy to come.

5. Please accept my sincere appreciation.

A. 敬赐复函

B. 期望你在百忙中光临

C. 请接受我真挚的感谢

D. 敬备菲酌，恭请光临

E. 恭请……

Task 2

Read the following passage about Business Invitation letter and Thank-you letters.

In business world, the most commonly used social writings are invitation cards and letters, and thank-you letters. They are mailed via post, and more often by email. Email has become the most commonly used way for business people to communicate with each other nowadays.

The **invitation letter** is one of the most popular ways of inviting relatives, friends, colleagues and business clients to important events. In a formal situation, an invitation letter refers to the request regarding the attendance of a prominent person, a group of people or representative of an organization at some particular event.

The features of effective letters are briefness and warmth. The tone of these letters is generally polite and semi-formal. For this letter, it should have an element of persuasion, as the purpose of the letter is not merely to invite but also to ensure that the recipient agrees to attend the event. It is a fine combination of present and future tenses where words and phrases are linked to present the content in an impressive manner.

Basically speaking, an invitation letter should contain the heading, date, inside address, salutation, body of letter, complementary close, signature and enclosures. But the content of the body is different from that of an application letter, which mainly focuses on the social event.

To begin with, you should tell the invitee what activities you'd like to invite him or her to take part in and why you'd like to invite him or her. Besides, you should also tell the invitee about the details such as time, place, attendants, your preparations, dress style, and so on.

Thank-you letters are frequently employed in social intercourse, for a thank-you letter can enhance personal and business relationships and can handsomely reward those who make a practice of sending them. If you are not sure whether a thank you is necessary, you err on the side of"necessary." Even when you have graciously thanked someone in person, a written thank you is often expected or required, or at the least, appreciated. In the business world, thank-you letters have become a must if you care about your career.

Usually, thank-you letters are in the informal style. It is not necessary to include an inside address, and a comma replaces the colon after the salutation.

🐧 Task 3

According to what you read about business invitation letters & thank-you letters, answer the following questions.

1. What is invitation letter?
2. How can you write an effective invitation letter?
3. What is composed of business invitation?
4. What is a thank-you letter?
5. How can you decline an invitation letter?

⭐ Part II   Sample Study & Writing Tips

Sample 1 Business Invitation

May 23, 2008

Dear Sir/Madam,

We would like to invite you to an exclusive presentation of our new digital cameras. The presentation will take place at Sheraton Hotel, at 9:00 a.m. on May 30. There will also be a reception at 10:30. We hope you and your colleagues will be able to attend.

China National I & E Corporation is a leading producer of high quality. As you well know, a recent technological advances have made products increasingly affordable to the public.

Our new models offer superb quality and sophistication with economy, and their new features give them distinct advantages over similar products from other manufacturers.

We look forward to seeing you on May 30. Just call our office at 4578210 and we will be glad to arrange a place for you.

Sincerely Yours,

Wang Wei

General Manager

China National I & E Corp.

Writing Tips

Wording of invitations should be conversational, as though the writer were extending the invitation orally. A general invitation should be cordial and sincere, while a formal invitation should be less personal, written in the third person.

Often formal invitations include "RSVP", which means "please let us know if you plan to attend," and a telephone number.

Regrets only: requires a reply only if the invited guest cannot attend. Invitations are written in the deductive pattern (direct way) and are relatively short.

Either kind of invitation must do three things:

➤ Invite the reader to the gathering.

➤ Offer a reason for the gathering.

➤ Give the date, time, and place of the gathering.

Task 1

Please complete the following invitation letter.

Dear Mr. Johnson,

    I take great pleasure in 1) _____ (邀请) you to an international sales conference 2) _____ (举行) at 10 am on 14 March 2004 at the 3) _____ (长城) Hotel.

    I hope that you will be able to 4) _____ (出席) the conference and 5) _____ (期待) meeting you there.

Yours sincerely,
John Clinton

Sample 2 Business Invitation

Dear Professor Smith,

On behalf of the Beijing Foreign Studies University and the English Teaching and Research Society, I would be very pleased to invite you to attend and give a presentation in the Conference on English teaching to be held in Beijing from October 25 to October 28, 2008.

You are an internationally famous English scholar and educator. Your participation will be among the highlights of the conference. We sincerely hope that you could accept our invitation. As you know, the participants of the conference are all college teachers and we plan to make it a truly academic meeting.

If you can come, please let us know as soon as possible, since we have to prepare the final program soon. We are looking forward to your acceptance.

Sincerely yours,
Denver

Writing Tips

    In writing business invitation, a simple background of the individual or company will suffice.

    In the body of the letter it is important to outline all of the information about the event. The date and time should be included as well as the theme and purpose for the event. At this point, a date should be mentioned in which guests should provide their reply by, and it may also contain any information regarding special roles played at the event, attire and items required for the guest to bring.

Be sure to mention any specifications about address code in the invitation letter.

Next, the appreciation for the guest to attend the party should be shown. This can be completed with a formal note, stating that you look forward to seeing the individual at the event. Remember, this needs to keep in tone with the rest of the letter.

The conclusion should contain the sign off and a line that ties the complete letter together, drawing the end of the invitation, with a salutation and a signature.

Task 2

Try to translate the Chinese into English.

Dear Mr. Pearson,

I am the 1) _____ (秘书) of a small business club in our city. We are organizing a reception for our business clients next Tuesday 23 May. We hope you will be able to 2) _____ (出席接待会) and give us a talk. I 3) _____ (将会很感激) if you could tell me which topic you are interested in.

The dinner will begin at 8:30pm and please 4) _____ (着装正式).
We will 5) _____ (承担一切花费) here and look forward to seeing you.

Yours sincerely.

Sample 3 Thank-you Letter

June 30, 2008

Dear Sir/Madam,

Thank you for your letter of June 28 inviting our corporation to participate in the 2008 International Fair. We are very pleased to accept the invitation and will plan to display our home electrical appliances as we did in previous years.

Mr. Li will be in your city from July 12 to 17 to make specific arrangements and would very much appreciate your assistance.

Yours faithfully,

Wang Hao

Writing Tips

Although in many cases, thanks could be conveyed as well by telephone calls, letters seem much more thoughtful. By writing letters of appreciation, you can show your respect for others.

A thank-you letter goes beyond simply thanking the receiver for being kind; it notes the consideration, the extra effort and the kindness extended. A thank-you letter converting business situation might be sent promptly. It also must sound sincere, be specific about that which is appreciated, and be short as well.

A proper thank-you letter should:

➢ Begin with a statement of thanks

➢ The rest includes details about the situation. Tell how useful or appropriate it is, how you plan to use it, where you have placed it (home, office, wardrobe) or how it enhances your life. Be specific about what pleased you.

➢ End with a positive and genuine statement.

🐧 Task 3

Decide which of the following statements of thanks will be used as the beginning the business thank-you letter.

1. I am writing to extend/convey my heart-felt thanks/sincere appreciation/gratitude to you for...

2. Please accept my gratitude, now and always.

3. I must thank you again for your generous help/kind assistance.

4. My true gratitude is beyond words. Thank you again.

🐧 Task 4

Write a positive and genuine statement for a thank-you letter.

_____

_____

⭐ Part III Vocabulary in Use

exclusive /ɪk'sklu:sɪv/	*adj.*	not divided or shared with others 独家的
presentation /ˌprezn'teɪʃn/	*n.*	the activity of formally presenting something (as a prize or reward) 陈述，介绍
digital /'dɪdʒɪtl/	*adj.*	of a circuit or device that represents magnitudes in digits 数字的
reception /rɪ'sepʃn/	*n.*	the act of receiving 招待，接待
colleague /'kɒli:g/	*n.*	an associate you work with 同事
technological /ˌteknə'lɒdʒɪkl/	*adj.*	based in scientific and industrial progress 技术上的
advance /əd'vɑ:ns/	*n.*	a movement forward 前进，推进
affordable /ə'fɔ:dəbl/	*adj.*	that you have the financial means for 付得起的
model /'mɒdl/	*n.*	a type of product 型号
superb /ˌsju:'pə:b/	*a.*	of surpassing excellence 极好的
sophistication /səˌfɪstɪ'keɪʃn/	*n.*	being complicated, refined （机器）的先进，精良

distinct /dɪ'stɪŋkt/	*adj.*	easily or clearly heard, seen, felt, etc. 清晰的；清楚的；明白的
manufacturer /ˌmænjʊ'fæktʃərə/	*n.*	a business engaged in manufacturing some product 制造商
highlight /'haɪlaɪt/	*n.*	the most interesting, important or memorable part 最重要，最精彩的部分
corporation /ˌkɔːpə'reɪʃn/	*n.*	business company 公司
display /dɪ'spleɪ/	*v.*	put sth on show 展示
previous /'priːviəs/	*adj.*	coming before in time or order 原先的
specific /spə'sɪfɪk/	*adj.*	detailed, precise and exact 具体的
appreciate /ə'priːʃɪeɪt/	*v.*	value highly 感激

Expressions

1. exclusive presentation 独家推介
2. digital camera 数码相机
3. take place 举行，发生
4. attend a reception 出席招待会
5. on behalf of 代表
6. accept the invitation 接受邀请
7. International Fair 国际商品交易会
8. participate in 参加
9. home electrical appliances 家用电器
10. make special arrangements 进行具体安排

Part IV   Practical Writing Tasks

Practice 1 Fill the blanks with the following information.

look forward to	helpful	assist	express
add	appreciation	greeting	

Dear Mr. Smith,

Thank you very much for 1) _____ our new colleague while she was in London. I know that she has already written to you, 2) _____ her gratitude, but I would like to 3) _____ my own 4) _____ . The introductions you made and the information she gained will be extremely 5) _____ .

We are 6) _____ the pleasure to 7) _____ you in Paris soon.

Yours sincerely,

Mark

Practice 2 Fill in the blanks with the words and expressions given bellow. Change the form where necessary.

contact	accept	invite	specific	pleased
fair	sorry	request	service	solve

1. Thank you for your letter of March 20 _____ our corporation to participate in the 1997 International Fair.

2. We are very pleased to _____ and will plan to display our electrical appliances as we did in previous years.

3. Mr. Li will be in your city from April 2 to 7 to make _____ arrangements and would very much appreciate your assistance.

4. Thank you very much for your invitation to attend the 1997 International _____ .

5. As we are going to open a repair shop in your city at that time, we are _____ that we shall not be able to come.

6. We are _____ that our technical staff assisted you so capably.

7. We would like you to know that it you need to _____ us at any time in the future.

8. Our engineers will be equally responsive to your _____ for assistance.

9. If we can be of _____ to you again, please let us know.

10. We greatly appreciate your letter describing the assistance you received in _____ your air-conditioning problems.

Practice 3 Translation

I. Translate the following sentences from Chinese into English.

1. 我公司将于 7 月 7 日主办晚会欢送 ABC 公司总裁王先生光荣退休。

2. 恭请于 2009 年 4 月 5 日晚 7 点光临。地点：湖州市康泰路 290 号湖州宾馆。

3. 王先生自从 1999 年就担任 ABC 公司总裁。自他任职以来，ABC 公司的业务蓬勃发展。

4. 现在我们可以利用这个机会感谢他的杰出领导，并祝贺他退休愉快。

5. 请和我们一起向王先生道别。

II. Translate the following sentences from English into Chinese.

1. Mr. And Mrs. Zhang Zhongliang request the pleasure of Ms. Ng Lai Si's company at the marriage of their daughter Zhang Ying to Mr. Dong Zhiqiang.

2. We take great honor in inviting you to attend the conference.

3. Let me express our thanks for your caring and support for our company all these years with which our business is expanded extensively.

4. Again, you are cordially invited to our company for review, guidance and intercourse and also a following-up banquet on next Thursday, 15th May.

5. Should you find it possible to accept this invitation, would you be kind enough to let me know the date and time when you would like to come?

Practice 4 Practical Writing
Write an invitation letter, using the following information.

preparing, celebrate the 20th anniversary of our company, efforts, our staff, our company, ranked as, five leading companies, in the same field, in scope, profits, our achievements, hold activities, invite you, our regular business partner, celebrating ceremony and activities, ceremony, at Lotus Hotel, at 9:18 a.m. on May 28, a reception at 10:30, attend, looking forward to your reply, Li Wei

_____
_____
_____
_____
_____
_____
_____
_____

Part V   Key Sentences for Reference

※ Please let me know as soon as possible if you can come and tell me when you will be able to do so.
如能来的话，早日告我，何时为宜。

※ Please confirm your participation at your earliest convenience.
是否参加，请早日告之。

※ We have decided to have a party in honor of the occasion.
为此我们决定举行一次晚会。

※ The reception will be held in …, on …
招待会定于……在……举行。

※ I take great pleasure in inviting you to …

　　我很荣幸邀请您……

※ I'm writing to invite you to …

　　我写信想邀请您……

※ We would appreciate it if you could confirm your participation at your earliest convenience.

　　如果您能早日确定是否参与，我们将不胜感激。

※ Many thanks for your kind invitation. I am very pleased to accept your invitation.

　　非常感谢您的诚挚邀请。我很高兴接受您的邀请。

※ I would like to attend … Unfortunately, I have to …

　　我很想出席……但遗憾的是，我不得不……

※ Please accept my sincere appreciation for …

　　请接受我对……真挚的感谢。

※ I am truly grateful to you for …

　　为了……我真心感激您。

※ It was good (thoughtful) of you …

　　承蒙好意（关心）……

※ You were so kind to send …

　　承蒙好意送来……

※ Thank you again for your wonderful hospitality and I am looking forward to seeing you soon.

　　再次感谢您的盛情款待，并期待不久见到您。

※ I sincerely appreciate …

　　我衷心地感谢……

※ I wish to express my profound appreciation for …

　　我对……深表谢意。

※ I am writing to extend my sincere gratitude for …

　　I am writing to show my sincere appreciation for …

　　I would like to convey my heartfelt thanks in this letter to you for …

　　我写信想表达我真挚的谢意。

※ I feel deeply indebted to you and I really don't know how to thank you enough for your help.

　　我感到诚挚的谢意，对您的帮助再怎么感谢也不为过。

※ I must thank you again for your help.

　　再一次表达对你的谢意。

※ My gratitude is beyond the word's description.

　　My gratitude to you is beyond words.

　　对您的谢意无法用言语表达。

※ My parents join me in giving you our heartfelt thanks.

　　我和我父母对您表达真诚的感谢。

※ I would like to express my gratitude / warm thanks to you (along with my best wishes).

我想要表达我最真诚的感谢。

※ But for your kind encouragement, I would never have achieved such success.

没有你的鼓励，我不可能取得成功。

※ Thank you so much for your valuable present.

非常感谢你珍贵的礼物。

※ Many thanks for your kind and warm letter.

非常感谢你热情洋溢的来信。

※ Please accept my sincere appreciation for your kind inquiry about my health.

您对我健康的真情询问，我非常感激。

※ I'm forever grateful for all your past kindness.

我永远都会感激您过去对我的真诚。

※ I hope something will bring you to New York soon so that I can reciprocate your kindness.

我希望您有机会来纽约，以便我报答您对我的真挚情谊。

Business Reports

Learning Objectives

To be proficient in

➤ understanding knowledge of business reports;
➤ using key terms, useful expressions and key sentences in business reports;
➤ writing business reports.

Part I   Warming-up Activities

 **Task 1**

Translate the following phrases into Chinese.

1. Informal Report
2. Formal Report
3. Memo Report
4. Letter Report
5. Feasibility Report
6. Accident Report
7. Investigative Report
8. Progress Report
9. Trip Report
10. Proposal Report

 **Task 2**

Read the following passage about business report and discuss how business report is written.

Business report is defined as a kind of writing used for exchanging information by companies and enterprises. It provides relative information and data for reference. It is the medium of exchanging information in and among business as well as the basis for most major or decisive sales, investment and marketing actions.

Business report is usually made up of facts and arguments on a specific subject. In a report, situations are analyzed, conclusions drawn, alternatives considered and recommendations made. It is widely used, involving finance, audit, profits and losses, investment, annual production, sales, market analysis, personnel, etc.

There are several ways to classify business reports. The most popular classification is by the degree of formality: Informal Report and Formal Report. Moreover, according to the form that a report takes, reports can be categorized as Memo Report, Letter Report and Short Document Report. According to the length of the reports, there are long report and short report. According to different contents, business reports can be classified into Feasibility Report, Accident Report, Investigative Report, Progress Report, Trip Report, Proposal Report, etc.

Task 3

Answer the following questions, according to what you read.

1. What is the purpose of writing a business report?
2. What is the layout of a business report?
3. What are the different types of business reports?

Part II   Sample Study &Writing Tips

An accident report is used to gather and record the details of an accident such as time, place, and chain of events. It explores the cause of the accident and raises solutions to it if possible.

Sample 1 Accident Report

To:Steven Green, Safety Officer

From:Gillian Miller, Foreman of Section 4, Workshop 2

Date: July 20, 2013

Subject: Personal-Injury Accident in Section 4, Workshop 2, June 10, 2003

Introduction

On June 10, 2013, while John Smith was examining the structure of the kitchen, a loosing plank dropping from the ceiling hit his head. If Mr. Smith had put on the safety helmet, this accident would have been prevented. To prevent further such accidents, I have asked workers to examine boards of all ceilings and warned all the people from this kind of accident.

Accident Description

On June 10, 2013, at 10:5 p. John Smith, supervising engineer, examined the ceiling structure of room 801 and was hit by a loosing plank dropping from the ceiling. The cornea of the eyeball was slightly injured. While an ambulance was being called, Jane Cullions, administered first aid.

The ambulance from Chaoyang Hospital came at 10 : 45 p. m. , and John Smith was admitted to the emergency room at the hospital at 11 p. m.. He was treated and kept overnight for observation, then released the next morning. And John Smith returned to work one week later, on June 17.

Conclusions About the Cause of the Accident

All planks should be fixed tightly and the quality of the building should be reexamined. At the same time, all people get inside the construction plant should wear safety helmet. However, John Smith ignored the safety regulations.

To prevent a recurrence of this accident, I have conducted a brief safety session with all construction workers and supervising engineers and stressed that all construction workers must wear the safety helmets while working.

Writing Tips

There are a few standard rules for writing business reports that dictate what information should come in which section of the report. This format is followed in most of the business report examples that one may refer to. The most widely used format consists of the following standard sections:

Title Section: In a short report, this could be the first page bearing the title of the report, author name and date. The reason of making such a report could also be included in this section, so that the reader can establish an instant connection with the information in subsequent sections. In case of long reports, include the Table of Contents, Terms of References and so on.

Summary: Give a very clear and precise information about the problem or aspect of business that the report is analyzing. Also, include the main points, conclusions, recommendations and important results.

Methodology: List the methodologies used in your research, like if you interviewed focus groups or consulted research firms. Also, give the reason why you resorted to using a particular methodology.

Introduction: This is the first part of a proper report. Use this section to provide the background of the report. Highlight the reasons why the report is important for the readers. Include information about what is covered in the main body and the order in which the details are covered in the report.

Main Body: This is the heart of the report. Arrange all the information in order of priority, so that this section follows a logical sequence. Divide this section further into subsections. Lend greater order to the Main Body using sub-titles within each subsection. A paragraph about the relevance of the findings of the report can also be included in this section.

Data Tabulation: Another important factor when writing format of business report is data tabulation. Presenting your data in lists or tables can help in readily understanding the report. Also, data tabulation or listing, makes the report look professional and neat. So, accompany necessary lists or tables in your report whenever required. Make sure you use neutral colors to make tables and keep the list and tables looking neat and crisp.

Conclusion: Present logical conclusions for the topic investigated in the report. One can also suggest an option for the way forward. In case, discussion has not been included in the Main Body, include it in the conclusion. Otherwise keep this section small.

Recommendations: Include those solutions in this section. List them in bullets and numbered lists for easier comprehension.

 # Sample 2 Investigative Report

 **Task 1**

Please try to complete the following report with the given Chinese.

To:Kim Kate, General Manager
From:Alice Young, Personnel Director
Date:March 1, 2013
Subject:Investigation of the possibility of working flextime

Introduction

1) _____

_____ (总经理指示我就弹性工作制的可行性撰写一份报告). 1000 questionnaires were issued, of which 856 were returned. A sheet summarizing the positive and negative responses as well as the possible core-time and different time-bands is listed.

Findings

A. Staff Needs:

1. The major finding from the questionnaires on their needs was that most of the working mothers needed to be free from 3 : 30 in the afternoons. For the the reasons of collecting of young children from school; preparing meals for the family between the hours of 5 and 7p.m., etc.

2. 2) _____ (刚搬家的员工和距离公司较远的员工), needed extra time to arrive punctually in the morning.

B. Staff preferences:

1. Approximately 60% of the staff would prefer to arrive later in the mornings. The periods ranged from 30 minutes to 3 hours later.

2. 25% of the staff would prefer to finish work earlier than at present. This ranged from 30 minutes to 90 minutes.

C. Core Times:

1. Checking on the validity, accuracy and urgency of forms, documents and applications sent to the firm requires an efficient and streamlined operation. Some members of staff need to be on hand to verify, cross-check and revise communications ready for signing and despatch. This contingency did not depend on all office staff being present for consultation.

2. 3) _____ (电话咨询信息及建议的高峰时段) was between the hours of 10 a. m. and 3 p. m.

3. 4) _____ (最闲时段为下午 3:00~5:00), when business calls fell away, and some work was left for the following morning.

Conclusions

A. There is a conflict between the 23% of staff who need to arrive earlier in the day and the 60% who would prefer to arrive later. Most of the paperwork needs to be done earlier to be filed, signed and despatched while senior staff are available and also to catch the earlier postal collections.

B. The 19% of staff—the working mothers—who need to arrive earlier and leave earlier would help to clear the backlog of work from the previous day, but they would need to be helped by extra staff.

C. There would need to be heavy discouragement of staff wishing to arrive 2 hours and more later than at present.

D. We would need to test the degree of certainty about late arrivals. Some staff are obviously not sure yet when they would prefer to arrive.

Recommendations

A. There should be the following time-bands:

1. 7:30 to 3:00

2. 8:00 to 3:30

3. 8:30 to 4:00

4. 9:00 to 4:30

5. 9:30 to 5:00

6. 10:00 to 5:30

7. 10:30 to 6:00

B. In the time bands (1) to (3) volunteers would be asked to bring the percentage up from 19% to 50%. Failing this, a compulsory rota system should be introduced in consultation with the staff associations and trade unions.

C. 5) _____ (所有员工必须在上午 10:30 至下午 3:00 之间在单位办公). This is the "core-time" we recommend.

D. 1. The needs of working mothers should have priority in early finishing.

2. The needs of those who live far away should have priority in late arrival time bands.

Sample 3 Periodical Report

🐧 *Task 2*

Please try to complete the following report with the given Chinese.

To: Robert Olson, Safety Director

From: Terry Miller, Safety Training Coordinator

Date: May 3, 2013

Subject: Safety Training Program for April 2013

Introduction

The training staff held one advanced training course for supervisory personnel and one basic training course for rank-and-file workers in April. 1) _____ _____ (5 月份，我们已经预订了一门高级课程和 两门基础课程) . Until enrollment increases, we will consolidate scheduled classes. The final version of the "Safety Manual", which is under revision, will be ready by May 10.

Work Performed During This Period

Two training sessions are not being well attended because 2) _____ _____ (这次培训是自愿参加). Unless this training is made compulsory, attendance will continue to be a problem.

Project Plans

The following classes are scheduled for May:

May 15 Advanced Course (Shop Superintendents and General Foremen)

May 22 Basic Course (Rank-and-file Workers)

May 29 Basic Course (Rank-and-file Workers)

Final editorial changes are being made in the Safety Manual. The cover, spine, section dividers, and final artwork for several drawings are nearing completion. 3) _____ _____ (手册将在 5 月 10 日前备好分发).

⭐ Part III   Vocabulary in Use

manuscript /'mænjʊskrɪpt/	n.	thing written by hand, not typed or printed 手稿
dictate /dɪk'teɪt/	v.	state or order sth with the force of authority 强行规定；指令；指定
bear /beə/	v.	be have 具有
subsequent /'sʌbsɪkwənt/	adj.	later; following 后来的；随后的
methodology /ˌmeθə'dɔlədʒi/	n.	a set of methods and principles used to perform a particular activity 方法学
resort /rɪ'zɔ:t/	v.	make use of sth for help; adopt sth as an expedient 求助于或诉诸某事物；采取某手段或方法应急或作为对策
highlight /'haɪlaɪt/	v.	give special attention to (sth); emphasize 对（某事物）予以特别的注意；强调
tabulation /'tæbjʊ'leɪʃən/	n.	a set or a list 表格
accompany /ə'kʌmpəni/	v.	be present or occur with sth 与某事物同时存在或发生
plank /plæŋk/	n.	long flat piece of sawn timber 木板
helmet /'helmɪt/	n.	protective head-covering 头盔
cornea /'kɔ:niə/	n.	transparent outer covering of the eye, which protects the pupil and iris 角膜
flextime /'fleksitaɪm/	n.	a system of working in which people work a set number of hours within a fixed period of time, but can vary the time they start or finish work 弹性工作时间
compile /kəm'paɪl/	v.	collect (information) and arrange it in a book, list, report, etc 收集（资料）并编辑（成书、表、报告等）
approximate /ə'prɔksɪmɪt/	adj.	almost correct or exact but not completely so 近乎正确或精确的；大约的；大概的
contingency /kən'tɪndʒənsi/	n.	event that happens by chance 偶发事件
rota /'rəutə/	n.	list showing duties to be done or names of people to do them in turn 勤务轮值表
rank-and-file	adj.	the ordinary members of an organization 普通成员

| consolidate /kən'sɔlɪdeɪt/ | *v.* | (cause sth to) become more solid, secure, or strong 使某事物巩固；加固；加强 |
| spine /spaɪn/ | *n.* | back part of the cover of a book, where the pages are joined together 书脊 |

Expressions

1. Informal Report 非正式报告
2. Formal Report 正式报告
3. Memo Report 便函体报告
4. Letter Report 书信体报告
5. Short Document Report 简短的文件体报告
6. Feasibility Report 可行性报告
7. Accident Report 事故报告
8. Investigative Report 调查报告
9. Progress Report 进度报告
10. Trip Report 公差报告
11. Proposal Report 建议报告
12. supervising engineer 监理工程师
13. safety session 安全会议

⭐ *Part IV   Practical Writing Tasks*

Practice 1 Terms
Match the following business English terms and phrases with their proper Chinese meaning.

1. letter of authorization	A. 附录部分
2. letter of transmittal	B. 简短文件体报告
3. list of illustrations	C. 前页部分
4. annual report	D. 年度报告
5. market analysis	E. 授权书
6. title fly	F. 标题页
7. title page	G. 标题衬页
8. short document report	H. 市场分析
9. preliminary part	I. 报告传达书
10. appended part	J. 插图目录

Practice 2 Fill in the blank with the words and expressions given bellow. Change the form where necessary.

presented	objective	distributed	aspect	mode
negative	collective	recommend	distribute	access

1. The _____ of this study is to provide information to determine which aspects of shopping environment cannot satisfy the customers, and to propose improvement solutions.

2. This report investigates the reasons for the problem and _____ measures for improvement.

3. The overriding problem with these is the _____ to the corporate website.

4. These cases had a _____ impact on our sales and the reputation of our market operator.

5. Up till now, the e-business company mainly falls into three groups: B2B, B2C, and C2C. The three _____ are different in making a profit.

6. Most of the information in this report was gathered from a questionnaire _____ to 45 IT workers, and from interviews with ten of them. Valid feedbacks in writing and interviews numbered 39.

7. The information of this report is gathered from interviews with directors of Bureau of Education for the Dongcheng and Xuanwu Districts, Beijing, and a _____ interview with 45 teachers from 15 schools in the two communities.

8. The cases _____ in the report was collected from some Chinese export and import companies based in Beijing.

9. The customer service staff _____ and collected the survey forms.

10. The customers are analyzed in various _____ , such as their age, sex, monthly income, and means of transportation.

Practice 3 Translation

I. Translate the following sentences from Chinese into English.

1. 本报告将介绍为实现这一目标而开设的有关课程。

2. 鉴于培训计划对实现公司的目的具有重要意义，我特此提出以下建议。

3. 这些问题还需要进一步的理解和协商，我们准备再次举行会议。

4. 此次出差的目的在于弄清 ABC 公司是否能够在一段时间内以固定的价格为我们提供橱柜。

5. 我准备起草一份会谈总结，将其以传真发给 ABC 公司，请他们做出修改后再用传真发回。

II. Translate the following sentences from English into Chinese.

1. These 50 interviews made in early July suggest that many aspects of the shopping environment in the Shopping City cannot satisfy the customers.

2. Facilities and services therefore need to be improved. The most noteworthy weaknesses are the lobby areas, toilet rooms, location signs, ventilating facilities, try-on cubicles and cashier services.

3. The visit was successful. The meetings and discussions with Yong Kang representatives led to a mutual agreement on several important issues.

4. I have asked workers to examine boards of all ceilings and warned all the people from this kind of accident.

5. The major finding from the questionnaires was that most of the working mothers needed to be free from 3: 30 in the afternoons.

> ※ You are the director of Training Department of ABC Company. You are drafting an investigative report on adopting English program for all senior employees with the aim of improving their English proficiency.
>
> ※ Describe the program and offer your conclusions and recommendations.

_____

_____

_____

_____

_____

_____

_____

_____

⭐ Part V   Key Sentences for Reference

※ A report has been requested by the Directors with the aim of finding possible ways to improve the popularity of Pitbank Fun Park.

本报告应董事会的要求作出，目的是探索提升彼畔游乐园知名度的方法。

※ The report is to be presented to the Directors as soon as possible.

本报告须尽快呈送董事会。

※ This report tries to find out who are the customers of ABC Center and whether they are satisfied with the services in the city.

本报告试图调查清楚谁是 ABC 中心的客户以及他们是否对本城市内的服务满意。

※ This report examines the extent of the problem of absenteeism among fourth-year Information majors at the university.

本报告旨在调查大学四年级信息专业学生旷课情况的严重程度。

※ In the past three months the Service Department received more than 100 complaints from surfers.

在过去的三个月中，服务部门收到了上网者 100 多个投诉。

※ From early this year, we have been receiving customer letters complaining about services of our sales persons.

从今年较早的时候起，我们就收到了关于我们销售人员服务方面的投诉信。

※ It has been found that more and more customers, especially foreign consumers, returned their goods bought in this supermarket.

我们发现已有越来越多的顾客，特别是国外顾客，退回在这个超市中购买的商品。

※ It is of vital importance to choose a suitable business mode and stay on it.

选择一种合适的模式并营运下来至关重要。

※ Some companies are inclined to change their business modes quite frequently, which have resulted in a waste of resources.

有些公司轻易频繁地变换他们的商务模式，这导致了资源的浪费。

※ Another key factor to set up an e-business company is the lack of continued investment.

建立电子商务公司的另一个因素是缺乏资金的持续投入。

※ The introduction and Background information was gathered from the Annual Report on China Export and Import.

导言和背景信息来源于中国进出口年度报告。

※ The information for this report was gathered from the questionnaires done by 100 students from University of International Business & Economics, who were chosen at random, including both undergraduates and postgraduates.

本报告的信息来源于对国际商务与经济大学 100 名同学做的问卷调查，他们是随机抽出的本科生和研究生。

※ The questionnaires were jointly designed by the marketing department, sales department and customer service department of MWB Bookstore.

问卷由 MWB 书店市场部、销售部和客户服务部共同设计。

※ The report investigates the structure of the customer groups. It also looks at customers' satisfaction and disaffection degree over the City's infrastructure, price and service.

这份报告调查了客户群的结构。它也分析了顾客对城市基础设施、价格和服务的满意和不满意的程度。

※ This report investigates the students' attitudes towards setting up a night snack bar.

这份报告调查了学生们对设立夜市小吃店的态度。

※ This report collects some detailed information about setting up the night snack bar.

本报告收集了关于建立夜市小吃店的详细资料。

※ The services are examined in two aspects: One is the infrastructures and facilities, and the other is the performance of shop assistants.

服务在两方面进行考查：一方面是基础设施和设备，另一方面是营业员的服务。

※ The three alternatives to fossil fuels considered in this report are solar energy, wind power and hydropower.

本报告中考虑的石油的三种代用品是太阳能、风电和水电。

※ From the figures presented in the findings, it can be concluded that :

从调查结果中的数据可以看出：

※ Revenue from new customers accounts for over 80 per cent of new business by the end of yesteryear.

到去年年末，来自新客户的收入占新业务的 80%。

※ Contracted sales agents have proved the most productive and cost effective in the direct marketing sector.

已签约的销售代理在直销领域证明是最有成效和低成本的。

Establishment of Business Relations

Learning Objectives

To be proficient in

➤ understanding knowledge for letters to business relations;
➤ using key terms, useful expressions and key sentences for letters to establish business relations;
➤ writing a letter for establishing business relations.

 **Part I   Warming-up Activities**

 **Task 1**

Find out what the following logos refer to with your partners.

Task 2

Read the following passage about the business request letter, and sum up the ways to organize your request letters.

A business request letter always asks for a specific action. It concisely describes what you want and details the action that you hope your recipient will take. It also thanks the recipient in advance for any special effort or favor needed to address your request. When you have to persuade a recipient to act on your request, emphasize the reasons for your request early in your letter. If you will accept several responses, then describe them and state which one you prefer. Carefully plan your request before writing your letter to prevent unreasonable demands, and then organize your request as follows.

1. Provide details regarding your past relationship with the recipient, if any, to help him remember you and take special notice. Next, tell the recipient why you are writing.

2. Tell the recipient what you want him to do and by when.

3. Provide the recipient with the information he needs to meet with your request, including any supporting documentation.

4. Offer to provide additional information to your recipient. Ask him to contact you to answer any questions or address any concerns about your request. Furnish your contact information, including your name and title, address, phone number, fax number and e-mail address.

5. Summarize your request and thank the recipient in advance for his assistance. Remain courteous and positive to the end.

Part II   Sample Study &Writing Tips

Sample 1 Request for Business

Gentleman,

We owe your name and address to the Citybank in Washington. As one of the leading exporters from the UK, we have excellent connections in the trade of furniture and are fully experienced in the export business for this kind of product through fifty years' business experience. We attach a catalogue and price list we are regularly exporting and trust some of these items will be of interest to you. We would be interested in receiving your inquiries for all kinds of furnitures, against which we will send you our quotations in sterling, FOB UK ports, packing included.

If you are not interested in consummating business of the import of our furnitures, please be good enough to forward this letter to the import corporations who may be interested in these items.

We look forward to your early reply with much interest.

Sincerely yours,

Jim Taylor

Sales Manager

Writing Tips

When writing the business letter with the aim of establishing business relations, make sure your letter well structured and your language polite. Basically, letters targeted at establishing business relations include the following five parts:

1) Stating the source of information, that is, making clear that how you learned the information of his company.

2) Introducing your own company briefly, including the business scope, products, service, trustworthiness and credit.

3) Identifying your intention of writing the letter, that is, establishing business relations.

4) Providing catalogue, such as, price list and samples.

5) Expressing expectations for a reply as a polite ending (expect to get the reply).

If it is the first letter delivered to the recipient, it should cover all the five parts. More detailed information can be provided if a specific request is made.

If the letter is written to decline a proposal, the convincing reason should be given. And it is better if the desire for further cooperation in other areas is expressed. If possible, you can recommend it to some other companies which may be interested. It is very important that the tone of the letter is positive and acceptable.

Sample 2 Request for Business

 *Task 1*

Please try to complete the following business letter with the given Chinese.

Dear Sirs,

Your company has been introduced to us by Freeman Co. Ltd., London, England, as a prospective buyer of Chinese silk. As this item falls within the business scope of our corporation, _____ (我们希望与贵公司早日建立业务关系).

To give you a general idea of the various kinds of silk now available for export, we attach a brochure. Quotations will follow upon receipt of your specific inquiry.

We look forward to hearing from you soon.

Your faithfully,
Jack Lee

Sample 3 Agreeing to Start a Business Relationship

Dear Sirs,

Your letter of November 21 addressed to our sister corporation in Shanghai has been transferred to us for attention. As the items fall within the scope of our business activities, we shall be pleased to enter into business relations with you at an early date. We have learned that you are one of the leading importers and wholesalers of textiles in Thailand.

We are exporters of the same lines of business, having a business background of some 40 years, and are now particularly interested in exporting to your country textiles of all types. All kinds of our products are good sellers and worth commendation for their excellent quality.

If you are interested in marketing these products at your end, please let us know and we shall be pleased to send you our quotations and sample books upon receipt of your specific inquiries.

Your faithfully,
Johnson Smith

 *Task 2*

Study the following letter and discuss with your partner on.

1. How can you decline a business quest?
2. What should we pay attention to when writing this kind of letters?

Dear Sirs,

Your letter of May 5 addressed to our Guangzhou Branch Office has been passed on to us and we feel thankful for your interest in cooperating with us.

However, we regret to inform you that this particular product has already been represented by Sam&Sam Co., 789 Broad Street, England. Therefore, we have to decline your suggestions since we are not in a position to offer you this goods any longer.

Should any other items be of interest to you, please let us know and we shall be pleased to make you offers.

Yours faithfully,
Pierre Davis

Sample 4 Transferring Business Relations

Dear Sirs,

Thank you for your interest in establishing business relations with us. We regret to inform you, however, that we do not manufacture furniture any longer. Our factory produces only boards which we sell to furniture manufactures.

Therefore, we are not in a position to offer you but would rather recommend to you a factory here that produces high-quality furniture and would be able to manufacture furnitures to your own design.

The address is: Songmu Furniture Corporation, 1 Huixin Street, Chaoyang District, 100021, Beijing, China.

We hope that this will be of help to you and wish you every success in your business dealings.

Yours sincerely,
Chen Meiyun

 Task 3

Discuss the following questions.

1. What information should be provided in a letter of transferring business relations?
2. What's the layout of this kind of business letter?

Part III   Vocabulary in Use

prospective /prə'spektɪv/   *adj.*   expected to be or to occur; future or possible 预期的；未来的；可能的

enlarge /ɪn'lɑ:dʒ/	v.	(cause sth to) become larger（使某物）变大；扩大；增大
turnover /'tə:nˌəuvə/	n.	the total amount of goods or services sold by a company during a particular period of time 营业额
attendance /ə'tendəns/	n.	action or time of being present 出席；到场；参加
periodical /ˌpɪəri'ɔdɪkə/	n.	a magazine that is published every week, month, etc. 期刊，杂志
catalogue /'kætəlɔg/	n.	complete list of items, usu in a special order and with a description of each 目录；目录册
decline /dɪ'klaɪn/	v.	refuse (sth offered), usu politely 拒绝（接受某物）；（通常指）谢绝
inquiry /ɪn'kwaɪəri/	n.	request for information (about sb/sth) 请求帮助；询问
consummate /'kɔnsəmeɪt/	v.	make (sth) complete or perfect 使（某事物）完整或圆满
forward /'fɔ:wəd/	v.	send (a letter, etc) to a new address 将（信件等）投递到新地址；转递
brochure /'brəuʃə/	n.	booklet or pamphlet containing information about sth or advertising sth（作介绍或宣传用的）小册子
manufacture /ˌmænju'fæktʃə/	v.	make (goods) on a large scale using machinery 用机器大量制造（货物）
represent /ˌreprɪ'zent/	v.	[尤用于被动语态] act as a substitute or deputy for (sb) 作为（某人）的代表或代理人

Expressions

1. Gentlemen 执事先生

2. attach a catalogue and price list 随附产品目录和价目表

3. forward this letter to 转递

4. business scope 经营范围

5. enter into business relations 建立业务关系

6. specific enquiry 具体询盘

7. sister corporation 姐妹公司

8. passed on to 转交

9. ...owe your name and address to... 从……处获悉贵公司的名称和地址

10. ...we will send you our quotations in sterling, FOB UK ports, packing included. 我们将给你方寄去我们的英镑 FOB 口岸价，包括包装价。

11. Quotations will follow upon receipt of your specific inquiry. 已收到贵方具体询价后，我方将进行报价。

12. ... has been transferred to us for attention. ……已转交给我方，并引起我方关注。

13. As the items fall within the scope of our business activities... 该项目属于我方业务范围……

14. we regret to inform you that this particular product has already been represented by... 我们很遗憾地通知你方，这款产品已由……代理。

⭐ *Part IV   Practical Writing Tasks*

Practice 1 Terms

Match the following business English terms and phrases with their proper Chinese meaning.

1. holding company   A. 总公司

2. conglomerate   B. 外商独资企业

3. joint venture (enterprise)   C. 联合大企业

4. state-owned enterprise   D. 母公司

5. private enterprise   E. 合资企业

6. exclusively foreign-owned enterprise   F. 控股公司

7. parent company   G. 私人企业

8. subsidiary company   H. 分公司

9. head office   I. 子公司

10. branch office/company   J. 国营企业

Practice 2 Fill in the blanks with the words and expressions given bellow. Change the form where necessary.

attention	exclusive	represent	possibility	delivery
inquiry	credit	line	consummate	expand

1. As to our _____ standing, you may refer to the Bank of China.

2. We have been for many years in the chemical _____ .

3. We are certain that business can be _____ between us.

4. We are sorry to inform you that we are fully _____ at this time.

5. Quotations and samples will be sent to you upon receipt of your specific _____ .

6. We are a state-operated company, handling _____ the import and export of cotton piece goods.

7. Your letter of March 5 addressed to our Dalian Office has been passed on to us for _____ and reply.

8. Should your price be found competitive and _____ date acceptable, we intend to place a large order with you.

9. In order to export our products to Western Europe, we are writing to you to seek cooperation _____ .

10. We thank you for your letter offering your services and should like to discuss the possibility of _____ trade between us.

Practice 3 Translation

I. Translate the following sentences from Chinese into English.

1. 经你方商会的介绍，我方欣悉贵公司的行名和地址。

2. 如果贵公司不进口上述产品，请将此信转给相关的公司。

3. 如对目录中所列之任何产品感兴趣，请具体询价，我方将立即报价。

4. 我们了解到你公司是中国手工艺品的出口商，因此冒昧地写信给你。

5. 为使贵方对我方所经营的产品有所了解，今特随函附寄产品目录及价目表，以供贵方参考。

II. Translate the following sentences from English into Chinese.

1. We shall appreciate your sending us a catalogue and price list by air immediately.

2. We have excellent connections in the trade and are fully experienced in the import business for this kind of product.

3. We are glad to hear from you and will carefully consider any proposals likely to lead to business between us.

4. We are interested in establishing business relations with your corporation for the purpose of supplying you the commodities you want.

5. We have learned from the Commercial Counselor's office of our Embassy to your country that you are one of the leading importers of electric and electronic equipment.

Practice 4 Practical Writing

Write a letter, using the following information:

Write a letter to Tom & Jack at Newton Street, London, E.C. 8, telling them that you wish to enter into business relations with them, with the following particulars:

※ Commented by British Chamber of Commerce;

※ The main line of business is exporting children's garments;

※ Ask Tom & Jack to give you the name of their reference;

※ Illustrated catalogue and price-list will be air-mailed against their specific inquiries.

_____

_____

_____

_____

_____

_____

_____

_____

⭐ *Part V   Key Sentences for Reference*

※ To give you a general idea of our products, we are sending you, under separate cover, our latest catalogue together with a range of brochures for your reference.

为了给贵方一个我们产品的总印象，我们将另函寄给你们一份最新产品目录以及一套小册子，供你们参考。

※ We trade in the import and export of textiles.

我们从事纺织品的进出口业务。

※ Your comments on packing have been passed on to our manufacturers for their reference.

你方对包装的建议已转交我方制造商参考。

※ We can assure you that your orders will receive our immediate and careful attention.

对你方所有的订单将予以及时认真办理。

※ The brochure attached will give you details of the varied service we can render.

随函附上小册子一本，向你方详细介绍我们所能提供的多种服务项目。

※ We have established business relations with firms of more than one hundred countries in the world.

我们已经和世界上一百多个国家商号建立了贸易关系。

※ Your letter dated 15th Feb. has been passed on to our Shanghai Office for attention and reply, as the goods you inquired for fall within the scope of their business activities.

你方 2 月 15 日函悉，并已转交给了上海分公司办理答复，因为你所询购的商品属于他们经营范围。

※ We are willing to enter into business relations with your company on the basis of equality and mutual benefits.

我方愿在平等互利的基础上与你公司建立贸易关系。

※ We have airmailed you some leaflets about our products.

我们已将有关产品的宣传单航空邮寄给贵方。

※ We mainly trade in the import and export of various light industrial products.

我们主要经营各种轻工业产品的进出口业务。

※ Our products are good in quality and favorable in price.

我公司的产品质量上乘，价格优惠。

※ We thank you for your letter of June 12 and should like to discuss the possibility of expanding trade between us.

谢谢贵方 6 月 12 日来函，我们愿就扩大贸易的可能性与你方进行讨论。

※ We understand that you are exporters of Chinese Arts & Crafts. We, therefore, are taking the liberty of writing you to repress our desire to enter into trade relations with you.

我们了解到你公司是中国手工艺品的出口商，因此冒昧地写信给你方，希望与你方建立业务关系。

※ Your letter dated 15th Feb. has been passed on to our Shanghai Office for attention and reply, as the goods you inquired for fall within the scope of their business activities.

你方 2 月 15 日函悉，并已转交给了上海分公司处理并答复，因为你所询购的商品属于他们的经营范围。

Business E-mail,
Fax and E-commerce

Learning Objectives

To be proficient in

➢ understanding knowledge of business E-mail, Fax and E-commerce;

➢ using key terms, useful expressions and key sentences for business E-mail, Fax and E-commerce;

➢ writing an E-mail, Fax and E-commerce.

Part I　Warming-up Activities

Task 1

Study the following picture and discuss the competitive advantages of this Internet commerce business.

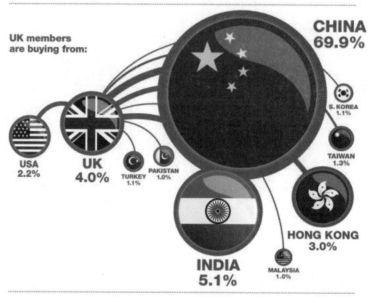

UK members are buying from:

CHINA 69.9%
S. KOREA 1.1%
TAIWAN 1.3%
HONG KONG 3.0%
MALAYSIA 1.0%
INDIA 5.1%
PAKISTAN 1.0%
TURKEY 1.1%
UK 4.0%
USA 2.2%

B2B-Directindustry

Task 2

Read the following passage about business E-mail, Fax and E-commerce. Discuss with your partners about other ways of Internet commerce business and their perspective advantages.

E-mail, short form for electronic mail, is a store and forward method of composing, sending, storing, and receiving messages over electronic communication systems.Being cheap, quick and easy, it is becoming more and more important in both business and in our personal lives as we are stepping into a no paper society.

Fax is a system for sending and receiving printed materials (such as documents and drawings) and photographs using telephone lines. Fax is especially useful when one is sending a signed document, drawings and charts, when a digital file of a hard-copy document is not available and when senders or recipients do not have access to a computer. Fax header is located at the top of the faxed pages. Fax header consists of the date and time of the transmission, the dialed fax number, the total pages in the file, the current page number and the sender's name. Fax header also indicates whether the fax machines send and receive the document successfully. The header format varies. For instance, the date and time may appear in the top right corner, while the top left corner often displays the pagination.

E-commerce, the abbreviation of electronic commerce, is a type of industry where the buying and selling of products or services is conducted over electronic systems such as the Internet and other computer networks. Electronic commerce is generally considered to be the sales aspect of e-business. It also consists of the exchange of data to facilitate the financing and payment aspects of business transactions. This is an effective and efficient way of communicating within an organization and one of the most effective and useful ways of conducting business.

Electronic commerce draws on technologies such as mobile commerce, electronic funds transfer, supply chain management, Internet marketing, online transaction processing, electronic data interchange (EDI), inventory management systems, and automated data collection systems. Modern electronic commerce typically uses the World Wide Web at least at one point in the transaction's life-cycle, although it may encompass a wider range of technologies such as e-mail, mobile devices, social media, and telephones as well.

Task 3

Answer the following questions according to what you've read.

1. What are the advantages of using E-mail and fax when establishing business relationships?
2. What are the differences between E-commerce and traditional commerce?

Part II   Sample Study & Writing Tips

Sample 1 E-mail

Subject: Arrival of Wolf Men's Dress Shirts
From:aaa@sohu.com
To:Calvin@hotmail.com

Dear Mr. Calvin,

We are happy to announce the arrival of Wolf's line of men's dress shirts from Italy. Made of pure silk and available at affordable prices, the shirts come in a variety of pleasing color tones. We invite you to stop by today and buy yours while supplies last.

Yours,

Tom

Writing Tips

With the development of Internet, more and more people use e-mail to do business on the Internet. E-mails are instant and easy to access, and it can save your cost and time. When writing an e-mail, you should bear in mind that:
1) The letter should be concise.
2) Use active voices instead of passive voices.
3) Use English colloquial form instead of written form.
4) Use more parallel structures.

 **Task 1**

Discussion: What are the principles of writing a business letter?

Sample 2 Fax

> 78 Qingnian Street,
> Dongcheng District
> Beijing, China
> Tel.: 6421 7478
> Fax: 6421 7479
>
> Mr. Clinton
> 20 Presidential Drive, Apartment A
> Wilmington
> Delaware, USA
> December 1, 2013
>
> Dear Mr. Clinton,
>
> It is a great pleasure to inform you that we have got all your ordered goods ready for shipment. Please establish your L/C at once. After receiving your L/C, we will effect the shipment of the goods as soon as possible.
>
> Yours faithfully,
> David Johnson
> Sales Manager, ABC Company

Writing Tips

1) Address is not always written out in full.

2) Each page of a fax should be clearly numbered.

3) The language used in faxed can be less formal than that in letters.

Task 2

Discussion: Study the following fax memo, and discuss its necessary elements with your partners.

> FAX TRANSMISSION
> DATE: _____
> TO: _____
> FAX NUMBER: _____
> FROM: _____

FAX NUMBER: _____

NUMBER OF PAGES TRANSMITTED INCLUDING THIS COVER SHEET:_____

MESSAGE: _____

Sample 3 Revision for Order

Task 3

Try to complete the following e-mail with the given Chinese.

SUBJECT: Revision for Order # 2010-11A

Dear Johns,

I'm sorry to inform you that I discovered an error in the order I sent you yesterday afternoon. 1) _____ (我打错了产品型号) for the leather jackets. It should correctly be #LJ-008, not #LJ-088 as I had originally indicated. 2) _____ (更改后的订单在附件中).I apologize for the 3) _____ (带来的不必要的不便).

Yours，
Jane

● Part III   Vocabulary in Use

compose /kəm'pəuz/	*v.*	write 写；创作	
indicate /'ɪndɪkeɪt/	*v.*	show sth, esp by pointing 指示；指出；标示	
pagination /ˌpædʒɪ'neɪʃən/	*n.*	the process of giving a number to each page of a book, magazine etc 标记页数	
facilitate /fə'sɪlɪteɪt/	*v.*	make (sth) easy or less difficult 使（某事物）容易或减少困难	
transaction /træn'zækʃən/	*n.*	transacting 办理；处理	
transfer /træns'fə:/	*n.*	transferring or being transferred 转移；转让；转录；调动	
encompass /ɪn'kʌmpəs/	*v.*	include or comprise sth 包含或包括某事物	
affordable /ə'fɔ:dbl/	*adj.*	inexpensive enough for people to afford 负担得起的	
effect /ɪ'fekt/	*v.*	cause to occur 使发生	
revision /rɪ'vɪʒən/	*n.*	a change or set of changes to sth 校订；修正	
leather /'leðə/	*n.*	material made by tanning animal skins 皮革	
indicate /'ɪndɪkeɪt/	*v.*	show sth, esp by pointing 指示；指出；标示	

Expressions

1. We are happy to announce the arrival of Wolf's line of men's dress shirts from Italy. 很高兴通知您意大利狼牌男士衬衫已到货。

2. at affordable prices 可接受的价格

3. The shirts come in a variety of pleasing color tones. 该衬衫现种类齐全，颜色多样。

4. stop by 莅临，顺便访问

5. effect the shipment 交货

6. I'm sorry to inform you... 很遗憾地通知您⋯⋯

7. It should correctly be... 应该为⋯⋯

Part IV   Practical Writing Tasks

Practice 1 Terms
Discuss the following terms with your partners and find out their respective advantages.

1. B2B

2. B2C

3. B2G

4. C2C

5. E-commerce

Practice 2 Fill in the blank with the words and expressions given bellow. Change the form where necessary.

detail	estimate	instruction	confirm	current
quote	transfer	prompt	inconvenient	expedite

1. Looking forward to a _____ reply.

2. The shipment is _____ to arrive at the Los Angeles port on July 3.

3. Please accept our apologies for an _____ this delay may cause you.

4. Your order will be supplied at the prices and terms stated in our _____ .

5. This e-mail is to _____ receipt of your order SST567, dated July 7.

6. Replying to your fax enquiry, we're pleased to airmail you an brochure for _____ information.

7. The exchange rate between RMB and USD is based on the day when you _____ the money.

8. Following your yesterday's E-mail _____ , we have today sent the subject order to you.

9. We regret that we are unable to ship your order by next month, as the specific items in your order are _____ out of stock.

10. We apologize for this unavoidable delay and would like to assure you that we are doing all we can to _____ shipping your order.

Practice 3 Translation

I. Translate the following sentences from Chinese into English.

1. 请参阅附上的电子目录。

2. 若能今早得到回复，我将不胜感激。

3. 此信的目的是想和贵公司在互利共同发展的基础上建立贸易联系。

4. 鉴于原材料价格浮动，该报价有效期不长。

5. 非常感谢贵方的电子邮件询价，我方很乐意给贵方寄去价格表。

II. Translate the following sentences from English into Chinese.

1. As we're able to make prompt delivery, we look forward to receiving our order by fax within the forthcoming week.

2. As soon as the goods are available, we'll inform you by fax.

3. Please confirm receipt of this order by e-mail or fax.

4. An irrevocable L/C will be established in your favor upon confirmation of order.

5. As you've indicated in your quote, we expect immediate delivery from stock.

Practice 4 Practical Writing
Write an E-mail, using the following information.

> ※ You are the sales manager of ABC Company. You saw an ad in the February issue of Clean Room magazine.
>
> ※ Write an e-mail of 120-140 words to the sales manager, requesting the brochure of their new products.

⭐ *Part V   Key Sentences for Reference*

※ A new fax number was set up.

新的传真号码已经设定。

※ Please notify me soon.

请尽快告知我。

※ Our quotation is valid for 90 days.

我们的报价 90 天内有效。

※ Please do not fail to write to me.

请一定回信。

※ Please refer to the attachment.

请查阅附件。

※ We are very pleased to know that you have the goods we want to order in stock and can make shipment in two weeks' time.

很高兴获悉我方想要订购的货物你方有库存，并且两周内就能发货。

※ Please email us when something new comes up.

有新情况请用电子邮件及时通知。

※ We're pleased to attach our current quotation for your reference.

欣然附邮时价表供你方参考。

※ The shipping documents, including the bill of lading, packing list and commercial invoice, will be sent via DHL tomorrow.

包括提单、装货清单及商务发票在内的装运单据明天将通过敦豪航空快递寄过去。

※ As an alternative, we would like to suggest sending the shipment to Los Angeles port.

作为一个备选方案，我们建议把货物运至洛杉矶港口。

※ Could you quote us the FOB price of the items below?

请将下列各项的船上交货价格报给我好吗?

※ Please provide us with an official quote for the items listed below.

请将下列各项的正式报价提供给我们。

※ Please let us know if you offer a volume discount.

请告诉我们你们是否提供批量折扣。

※ Your quote should include available discounts, a delivery schedule and payment terms.

你们的报价要包括可给折扣、交货日期以及支付条件。

※ If your prices are agreeable, we would be happy to place our first order.

如果你们的价格合适，我们会乐意下我们的第一份订单。

※ We will send you our official quote within three days after discussing your request with our factory.

我跟我们工厂商议一下您的要求后，会在三天内把正式报价发给您。

※ Actual delivery date will depend on the date of your order.

实际的交货日期将取决于您的订货日期。

※ A 50% deposit is required to process the order.

处理您的订单您需要先交 50% 的定金。

Business Circular Letters and Sales Letters

Learning Objectives

To be proficient in

➢ understanding knowledge of circular letters and sales letters;

➢ using key terms, useful expressions and key sentences for circular letters and sales letters;

➢ writing circular letters and sales letters.

Part I Warming-up Activities

Task 1

Translate the following sales promotion ways into Chinese.

1. International Chamber of Commerce

2. International Monetary Fund (IMF)

3. UN Conference on Trade and Development (UNCTD)

4. Organization for Economic Cooperation and Development (OECD)

5. World Trade Organization (WTO)

6. Council for Mutual Economic Aid (CMEA)

7. Association of South East Asian Nation (ASEAN)

8. International Investment Bank

9. Asia-Pacific Economic Cooperation (APEC)

10. International Finance Corporation (IFC)

Task 2

Read the following passage about the business circular letter & sales letter and tell the purpose of writing such letters.

A circular letter, somewhat general in topic, is used to share the same information with a large audience. It differs in purpose from a personal letter, which sends particular information to one or a few recipients. Circular letter includes internal and external letter. An internal circular letter is often used to announce new information or to clarify policies. While, an external one would be a letter circulated to all clients or to the public.

A sales letter is a type of business correspondence. A sales letter usually introduces new products and services, outlines a current sale, offer or promotion, or introduces an existing business to new customers or markets. This business letter can range from very formal to totally informal, depending on the industry, the audience and the type of promotion. Generally speaking, sales promotion consists of three forms: sales letter, reviver and follow up letter. Both the sales letter and reviver are usually written in the form of circular letter.

Task 3

Answer the following questions according to what you read.

1. What is the difference between a personal letter and a circular letter?

2. What is the purpose of an internal circular letter?

3. What are the three forms of sales letters? What is their function?

Part II   Sample Study & Writing Tips

Sample 1 Circular letter

October 23, 2013

Board Hosts Financial Education Day

High school students from Washington, D.C., learned about personal budgeting, responsible borrowing, and financing secondary education at workshops taught by Federal Reserve Board staff members on Wednesday.

The sessions at Francis L. Cardozo Senior High School and Columbia Heights Educational Campus were part of Federal Reserve Financial Education Day. Reserve Banks conducted more than 25 similar events for students and teachers around the country, highlighting the importance of financial education for young people.

"Financial education supports not only individual well-being but also the economic health of our nation," said Federal Reserve Chairman Ben Bernanke. "Effective financial education is not just about teaching students about financial products or performing financial calculations. It also involves teaching them the essential skills and concepts they will need to make major financial choices."

Federal Reserve Financial Education Day events drew on a series of four classroom lesson plans, "Financial Fundamentals from the Fed," that teach topics including earning income, saving and budgeting, use of credit, and financial institutions and services. The lessons are free, classroom-tested, and ready for use in high schools. For more information about the lesson plans and the Federal Reserve's other financial education resources, visit www.federalreserveeducation.org.

For media inquiries, please call 202-452-2955.

Writing Tips

When you are going to write a circular letter, there are several points for you to remember.

1) Know your audience. For circular letters, readership is diverse, so it can be difficult to gauge your audience's level of prior knowledge or familiarity with the content that you want to share.

2) Distinguish between internal and external circular letters. An internal circular letter, although circulated to a large group, is still restricted to a group. For instance, a business may circulate an internal letter to employees about a new company policy. In contrast, an external letter would be a letter circulated to all clients or to the public.

3) Use the tone and voice appropriate for the kind of communication (internal or external) for which the circular letter will function.

4) Share only authorized information.

 **Task 1**

Complete the following circular letter with the given Chinese.

October 23, 2013

To: All employees,

It has been observed very frequently that most of the employees are REGULARLY coming late to office. A few members of the staff have also 1) _____ (旷工) without any prior intimation for reason of their absence. The management has 2) _____ _____(严密关注)of the above. Please note the following as a strict warning:

1. LATE COMING : Any Employee's coming late by more than 5 minutes except 3 times will be marked absent for half the working day and salary will be deducted for the subsequent period.

2. SHORT LEAVE : only two short leaves are allowed in a month. The duration of one short leave is two hours. This can be taken any time during a day with prior information toHR Department by giving leave application form duly signed by the authorized signatory.

3. LEAVE APPLICATION: 3) _____ (任何未经事先批准的离开) or information will be marked absent for the day, leave application must be given in advance before taking any type of leave to HR department. This leave application is to be signed by the authorized signatory. If any one fails to do so, then absent will be marked and salary for the same will be deducted for the entire absent period. 4) _____ (在特殊情况下), the leave shall be granted without any prior information but the person has to 5) _____ (立即填写请假表)once he resumes his duties. In this case a telephone call is mandatory.

All are requested to kindly follow above.

Sample 2 Unsolicited Sales letter

Dear Ms. Linda,

We are sure that you would be interested in the new"Autumn Sun" solar-powered water heater, which is to be placed on the market soon. Most of the good points of the earlier types have been incorporated into this machine, which possess, besides, several novel features that have been perfected by years of scientific research.

The special advantage it offers will make it quick-selling line, and we are ready also to co-operate with you, by launching a national advertising campaign. Moreover, we are ready to assist to the extent of half the cost of any local advertising.

You will find enclosed leaflets describing this solar-powered water heater and we look forward to your reply.

Sincerely,

Tang Song

Writing Tips

A good sales letter consists of four essential elements: arouse interest, create desire, carry conviction and induce action.A sales letter needs to state more than "Buy our product. It's great." Knowing your prospect, using case studies and issuing a call to action are key elements of any good sales letter. Using these time-tested methods will keep your sales letter out of the circular file and turn more prospects into customers. Follow these steps to learn more.

1) Use a strong headline or heading that states the most important benefit you are offering to catch readers' attention and arouse their interest.

2) Highlight superiorities of the company and benefits (focusing on prices, quality, discounts)customers will get to stipulate their desire. Offer them solution to a problem to appeal to the reader's emotions. Tell them what you can do for them.

3) Design the letter for maximum visual impact.

4) Personalize your sales letter.

5) End with a call to action.

An unsolicited letter is to gather facts about products or service as well as identify several selling features that will fulfill specific customer needs. While, a solicited sales letter is an answer to an inquiry.

🐧 Task 2

Complete the following solicited sale letter with the given information.

Dear Mr. Short,

As requested in your inquiry of 26 June, 2013, we enclose a copy of our latest illustrated catalogue of hand bags.

_____

_____

_____

1) 很高兴贵方对我公司 "春" 系列手袋感兴趣。
2) 为鼓励贵方购进这款手袋，我方特对 20,000 美元以上的订单给予 10% 的优惠。

We look forward to a trial order. This would enable you to see for yourself the high quality and elegant taste of the hand bags.

Yours faithfully,

Jammy Steward

Sample 3 Reviver letter

Dear Mr. Harrison,

Looking through our record we note with regret that from July to October last year you bought a large quantity of copying machine from us. But recently, we didn't have the pleasure of an order from you.

We think you may be interested to know that we have a residue stock of 408 sets copying machine which you bought from us in substantial quantity previously. We are prepared to clear the stock by allowing you a generous discount of 5% on the current price. This offer is subject to your reply reaching here at the end of next month.

We look forward to your reply with earnest.

Yours faithfully,
Zhang Mei

Writing Tips

Reviver letter aims to retain or regain old customers instead of acquiring new ones. It is often written in the form of a circular letter. It is essential that in drafting a circular the following rules should be observed:
1) Keep the letter short.
2) Catch the reader's interest in the opening paragraph.
3) Give the letter an attractive look and make it as personal as possible.

 ## Task 3

Discussion: What is the layout of a reviver letter?
Sample 4 Follow-up letter

Mr. Truner,

We wrote you on February 16th in reply to your inquiry for washing machine. However, up to the present writing, we have not the pleasure of hearing from you. Your silence leads us to think that there must be something that prevents you from placing order with us.

Perhaps it is because you could not find the model you require from the catalogue sent by us. Now we enclose a copy of our newest catalogue. If any of the items illustrated in the catalogue interests you, please do not hesitate to let us know. We will make you offers upon receipt of your detailed requirements. We sincerely hope to conclude some satisfactory transaction with you in the near future.

We are most anxious to serve you and hope to hear from you soon.

Yours sincerely,
James Prior (Sales Manager)

Writing Tips

A follow-up letter will refer to the customer's inquiry and refer to the offer the firm has previously made. It will express regret or surprise that no order has been received and discreetly inquire into the reason. It is useful, wherever possible, to put forward in the follow-up letter new points and arguments favorable to the promotion of sales and the letter will end with the repeated hope that the customer will take advantage of the offer.

Task 4

Discussion: What are the differences between a reviver letter and a follow-up letter?

Part III   Vocabulary in Use

correspondence /ˌkɔrɪ'spɔndəns/	n.	letter-writing; letters 通信；信件
promotion /prə'məuʃən/	n.	advertising or other activity intended to increase the sales of a product（为推销商品而作的）广告宣传；推销活动
stern /stə:n/	adj.	serious and grim, not kind or cheerful; expecting to be obeyed 严肃的；严厉的
tardy /'tɑ:di/	adj.	slow to act, move or happen 行动缓慢的；拖拉的
absenteeism /ˌæbsən'ti:ɪzəm/	n.	the fact of being frequently away from work, especially without good reasons 旷工
confidential /ˌkɔnfɪ'denʃəl/	adj.	to be kept secret; not to be made known to others 恪守秘密的；机密的
superiority /su:ˌpɪəri'ɔrɪti/	n.	the state or quality of being better, more skilful, more powerful, greater, etc. than others 优势
stipulate /'stɪpjuleɪt/	v.	state (sth) clearly and firmly as a requirement 讲明
bombard /bɔmˌbɑ:d /	v.	attack with bombs 轰炸
solicitation /səˌlɪsɪ'teɪʃən/	n.	the act of asking someone for money, help, or information 恳求；诱惑
discard /dɪs'kɑ:d/	v.	throw (sth) out or away 扔掉，丢弃
budget /'bʌdʒɪt/	n.	estimate or plan of how money will be spent over a period of time, in relation to the amount of money available 预算
session /'seʃən/	n.	meeting 会议，集会
intimation /ˌɪntɪ'meɪʃən/	n.	(formal) the act of stating sth or of making it known, especially in an indirect way 暗示，通知
deduct /dɪ'dʌkt/	v.	take away (an amount or a part) 减去；扣除
subsequent /'sʌbsɪkwənt/	adj.	later; following 后来的；随后的

duly /'dju:li/	adv.	at the due and proper time; punctually 按时地；适时地；准时地
sanction /'sæŋkʃən/	n.	permission or approval for an action, a change, etc （对某种行动、变化等的）认可，批准
resume /rɪ'zju:m/	v.	continue (sth) after stopping for a time（停顿后）继续进行（某事物）
residue /'rezɪdju/	n.	what remains after a part or quantity is taken or used 剩余物
substantial /səb'stænʃəl/	adj.	large in amount; considerable 数目大的；可观的

Expressions

1. circular letter 通函

2. unsolicited sales letter 销售邀约函

3. solicited sales letter 征求销售函

4. reviver letter 振兴函

5. follow-up letter 随访函

6. personal budget 个人预算

7. Federal Reserve 美联储

8. enclose a copy of 随函附上

9. classroom-tested 课堂测试过的

10. resume one's duties 继续上班

11. All are requested to kindly follow above. 敬请大家遵照上述要求执行。

12. solar-powered water heater 太阳能热水器

13. novel features 新颖的特点

14. ...launching a national advertising campaign 开展全国性的广告宣传

15. enclosed leaflets 随附的宣传页

Part IV　Practical Writing Tasks

Practice 1 Discussion

Look at following pictures and discuss with your partners about different ways of promotion .

Practice 2 Fill in the blank with the words and expressions given bellow. Change the form where necessary.

requirements	place	absolutely	trial	recommend
illustrated	stock	subject	promising	locality

1. We have run out of _____ .

2. We enclose an _____ catalogue of our new items for your information.

3. You can use your products for two weeks _____ free.

4. We hope that you can help us promote the sales of this new product at your _____ .

5. Our new items are all nicely designed and would have a _____ market at your end.

6. We can maintain this reduction only for a short time, so we _____ your early orders.

7. If you will let us know the exact details of your _____ , we will do our utmost to meet your needs.

8. If you would like to _____ an order or receive more information, please log onto our website.

9. A comparison will convince you of the superb quality of our curtains and you shall find it is to you advantage to place a _____ order with us.

10. In order to popularize these products, all the catalogue prices are _____ to a special discount of 10% during the month of May only.

Practice 3 Translation

I. Translate the following sentences from Chinese into English.

1. 这项产品是我们最新的技术成果。

2. 非常感谢贵公司长期以来选择我们的产品。

3. 由于优良的质量，这个产品在欧洲大受欢迎。

4. 由于价格公道，工艺精湛，设计独特，我方的产品在年轻人中很受欢迎。

5. 由于此产品供不应求，兹建议从速决定，尽早惠赐订单。

II. Translate the following sentences from English into Chinese.

1. You can try our newly-developed cell phone for two weeks absolutely free.

2. This products is highly praised and appreciated by the customers at home and abroad.

3. We deem it to your advantage to buy this item for a trial sale in your market.

4. We give you this special discount for the order with the view of developing the business relations between us.

5. We believe that the above terms are acceptable to you and await your final order with keen interest.

Practice 4 Practical Writing
Write a sales letter , using the following information.

※ You are supposed to promote the new model of packaging machine.

※ Write a sales letter of 120-140 words to Mr. Farmer, manager of C&C Company, highlight superiorities of the product and benefits customers will get to stipulate their desire.

※ Write your sales letter in a conversational style and make sure to include all of your contact information—telephone number, fax number, email address, postal address, and your website address.

_____

_____

_____

_____

_____

_____

_____

_____

Part V   Key Sentences for Reference

※ We have at present only 50 metric tons of walnut meat in stock.
我们目前只有 50 吨核桃仁现货。

※ Only Type 12 is in stock. Type 18 is out of stock.
仅 12 型有货，18 型已卖完。

※ We are well stocked with men's shirts of different sizes.
我方备有充足的各种尺码的男式衬衫。

※ If for any reasons, you find our products unsuitable to your needs, we will replace your order or refund you.
如若不满意，我方将为您退换产品或退款。

※ We are sending you our revised catalogue and price-list, containing quotations for large orders taken from our existing stock.

现寄上新修改的目录和价目表，并附有批量订购现货的报价。

※ We would particularly like to draw your attention to our new set of greeting cards, which you will find on page 8 of the catalogue.

特别希望您能注意一下目录第 8 页上那一系列新的贺卡。

※ Although we sent you our catalogue on March 9th we have not received any orders from you, and we should like to know if there is any additional information you require about our products.

尽管我们 3 月 9 日给你们寄去了目录本，但却没有收到你方订单。我们想知道你方是否需要了解有关我方产品的其他信息。

※ You will note that we are making you a special reduction in prices owing to your support in the past.

您会注意到，由于贵方在过去给予我们的支持，我们特别给你们降价。

※ For an old customer like you, we are willing to allow a 5% commission on each machine, plus a discount of 8% on all orders received before the end of this month.

对于您这样的老客户，我们愿意对每一部机器给 5% 的佣金，此外对于在本月底之前收到的订单我们还给 8% 的折扣。

※ We are sending you a price-list and full sales promotion literature for your reference.

我们将会为您提供一个价格表和完整的促销刊物以供您参考。

Business Letters of Credit

Learning Objectives

To be proficient in

➢ understanding knowledge of letters of credit;
➢ using key terms, useful expressions and key sentences for letters of credit;
➢ writing a letter of credit.

Part I   Warming-up Activities

Task 1

Read the following dialogue and discuss the meaning of the italicized phrases with your partners.

Roger:　Well, we've settled the question of price, quality and quantity. Now what about the terms of payment?

Grey:　We only accept payment by *irrevocable letter of credit* payable against shipping documents.

Roger:　I see. Could you make an exception and accept *D/A or D/P* ?

Grey:　I'm afraid not. We insist on *a letter of credit*.

Roger:　To tell you the truth, a letter of credit would increase the cost of my import. When I open a letter of credit with a bank, I have to pay a deposit. That'll tie up my money and increase my cost.

Grey:　Consult your bank and see if they will reduce the required deposit to a minimum.

Task 2

Read the following passage about business letters of credit and answer the questions below according to what you have read.

A letter of credit (L/C) is a document issued by a financial institution, or a similar party, assuring payment to a seller of goods and/or services provided certain documents have been presented to the bank. These are documents that prove that the seller has performed the duties under an underlying contract and the goods have been supplied as agreed. In return for these documents, the beneficiary receives payment from the financial institution that issued the letter of credit. The letter of credit serves as a guarantee to the seller that it will be paid regardless of whether the buyer ultimately fails to pay. In this way, the risk that the buyer will fail to pay is transferred from the seller to the letter of credit's issuer. The letter of credit can also be used to ensure that all the agreed upon standards and quality of goods are met by the supplier, provided that these requirements are reflected in the documents described in the letter of credit.

Letters of credit are used primarily in international trade for transactions between a supplier in one country and a customer in another. The parties to a letter of credit are the supplier, usually called the beneficiary, *the issuing bank*, of whom the buyer is a client, and sometimes an advising bank, of whom the beneficiary is a client. Almost all letters of credit are irrevocable, i.e., cannot be amended or canceled without the consent of the beneficiary, issuing bank, and confirming bank, if any.

The relative parties in a documentary credit: applicant(opener), opening bank or issuing bank, advising bank or notifying bank, beneficiary, the confirming bank, negotiating bank, the accepting bank, paying bank, the reimbursing bank.

Step 1: A buyer and a seller enter into a sales contract providing payment by a documentary credit.

Step 2: The buyer instructs the issuing bank to issue a documentary credit in favor of the seller.

Step 3: The issuing bank opens a documentary credit according to the instructions of the applicant.

Step 4: The issuing bank asks another bank, usually in the country of the seller, to advise and perhaps also to add its confirmation to the documentary credit.

Step 5: The seller examines the documentary credit, and requires an amendment of the credit if necessary.

Step 6: The seller examines the documentary credit and prepares for the required documents.

Step 7: The seller presents his documents to the advising bank for settlement.

Step 8: The negotiating bank forwards documents to the issuing bank, claiming reimbursement as agreed between the two banks.

Step 9: The issuing bank examines the documents and reimburses the negotiating bank.

Step10: The buyer redeems the documents and picks up the goods against the documents.

Question 1. What's the function of a letter of credit?

Question 2. How many parties are involved in a letter of credit?

Part II   Sample Study &Writing Tips

Sample 1 Letter of Credit

Hong Kong and Shang Hai Banking Corporation

London, England

Irrevocable Documentary Credit No. 601

Date and Place of Issue: February 15, 2013, London

Date and Place of Expiry: April 10, 2013, London

Applicant: ABC Co. London, England

Beneficiary: China National Electronics Import and Export Corporation

Advising Bank: Bank of China, Beijing

Amount: € 20,000 (say twenty thousand Euro only)

Shipment: From China Port to London, middle March, 2013. Partial shipments and transshipment are prohibited. Credit available by the documents detailed herein and by your draft at sight for full invoice value.

—Signed Commercial Invoice in quadruplicate.

—Full set of clean on Board Ocean Bills of Lading made to order and blank endorsed marked "Freight Prepaid".

—Insurance Certificate or Policy for full invoice value Plus 10%, covering against All Risks and War Risks on 1000 washing machines.

Covering 1000 washing machines of WEILI at € 500 each CFRC 3% London.

As per Contract No. 601

Writing Tips

At present, most L/Cs are opened by telecommunication. Although the forms are different, their contents are, in the main, the same. The following details are to be found on all credits.

1) Name and address of the issuing bank.

2) Type of the credit. Every credit must indicate whether it is revocable or irrevocable. Whether it is a transferable credit or a confirmed credit must also be indicated in the credit.

3) Name and address of the beneficiary.

4) Amount of the credit and its currency.

5) Expiry date of the credit and its place to be expired.

6) Name and address of the applicant.

7) L/C number and date of issue.

8) Drawer and drawee as well as tenor of the draft. The drawer is always the beneficiary, the drawee may be the issuing bank or any other bank.

9) Full details of the goods.

10) Full details of the documents to be presented.

11) Partial shipment permitted/not permitted.

12) Transshipment allowed/not allowed.

13) Port of shipment and port of discharge.

14) Latest date for shipment, and the latest date for presentation of documents.

15) Instructions to the advising bank, negotiating bank or paying bank.

16) Other special terms and conditions.

17) The undertaking clause of the issuing bank.

Task 1

Discussion: Study the above letter of credit and discuss with your partners on the layout of a letter of credit.

Sample 2 Urging the Establishment of L/C

Dear Sir / Madam,

Re: Urging the Establishment of L/C

With reference to the 1000 pieces of Su embroideries under the Sales Confirmation No. SE113, we wish to draw your attention to the fact that the date of delivery is approaching, but your L/C has not been received by us. Please do your utmost to expedite its establishment so that we may execute the order within the prescribed time.

We look forward to receiving your response at an early date.

Yours sincerely,
Steven

Task 2

Study the above business letter of urging the establishment of L/C, and complete the following business letter of confirmation of the establishment of L/C with the given information.

Dear Sir / Madam,

Re:Order No. SE113

_____

_____

_____

1) 我方已在苏格兰皇家银行开立贵方为受益人的信用证，总金额为 60,000 英镑，有效期至 12 月 30 日。

2) 该信用证由中国银行苏州分行保兑，他们将接受贵方汇票总额，见票即付。

The documents required for negotiation are: 3 Commercial Invoices, 2 Bills of Lading and Insurance Policy.

Please advise us by fax when the embroideries have been shipped.

Sincerely yours,

Linda

Sample 3 Request for amendment to the L/C

Task 3

Please try to complete the following letter with the given Chinese.

Dear Sirs,

Re:L/COrder No. 329 issued by Citibank, California

We wish to acknowledge receipt of your L/C No. 329, covering your order for 2000 dozen of Men T-shirts. On perusal,1) _____ (我们发现一些差错). Please amend the L/C as follows:

1. The name of the goods are"Men T-shirts" instead of "T-shirts".

2. The unit price should be"200 RMB" instead of "200 pound".

3. "Draft to be at sight" should be instead of 2) " _____ (交单后 60 天付款)".

Your early fax amendment to the L/C will be highly appreciated.

Faithfully yours,

Susan

 # Sample 4 Requesting Extension of L/C

Task 4

Please try to complete the following letter with the given Chinese.

Dear Sirs,

Re: Requesting Extension of L/C

We appreciate your L/C No. 123 dated 30th July, covering your order for Type T2 keyboards. According to our Sales Confirmation, 1) _____ (我们应该在下周交货). However, we are regretful to inform you that the shipment here is paralyzed due to the sudden typhoon on Thursday. It is reported that the shipment cannot be recovered until the end of this month. Therefore, we request you to extend the shipment date to 15th August, and 2) _____ (信用证有效期延至 8 月 30 日).

Please accept our apology and amend your L/C.

Sincerely yours,
Tom Green

⭐ Part III   Vocabulary in Use

deposit /dɪ'pɔzɪt/	*n.*	pay (sth) as part of a larger sum, the rest of which is to be paid later 付（定金）
consult /kən'sʌlt/	*v.*	go to (a person, book, etc.) for information, advice, etc. 请教（别人）
ultimately /'ʌltɪmɪtli/	*adv.*	in the end; finally 最后，最终
irrevocable /ɪ'revəkəbəl/	*adj.*	that cannot be changed or revoked; final 不能改变的；不能撤回的；不能取消的
issue /'ɪʃu:/	*v.*	to officially make a statement, give an order, warning etc 发行
expiry /ɪk'spaɪəri/	*n.*	ending, esp. of the period when a contract or agreement is in force 终止，届期，期满，满期（尤指合同或协议的有效阶段）
partial /'pɑ:ʃəl/	*adj.*	of or forming a part; not complete 部分的；不完全的
transshipment /trans'shipment/	*n.*	to transfer for further transportation from one ship or conveyance to another 转车，转运
prohibit /prə'hɪbɪt/	*v.*	forbid sth or sb from doing sth esp. by laws, rules or regulations 禁止某事物或禁止某人做某事
herein /ˌhɪər'ɪn/	*adv.*	in this place, document, statement or fact 在此处，鉴于
quadruplicate /kwɔ'dru:plɪkət/	*n.*	in four exactly similar examples or copies 一式四份

endorse /ɪn'dɔːs/	v.	write one's name on the back of (esp. a cheque) 在(尤指支票）的背面签字；背书
embroidery /ɪm'brɔɪdəri/	n.	a design of colored stitches on cloth 刺绣
expedite /'ekspɪdaɪt/	v.	hasten or speed up 加快；加速
execute /'eksɪkjuːt/	v.	carry out, perform (what one is asked or told to do) 执行；实行；履行；完成
prescribe /prɪ'skraɪb/	v.	declare with authority that (sth) should be done or is a rule to be followed 规定做（某事）；指定遵守（某事物）
paralyze /'pærəlaɪz/	v.	to make something unable to operate normally 使瘫痪

Expressions

1. applicant(opener) 开证申请人
2. opening bank or issuing bank 开证行
3. advising bank or notifying bank 通知行
4. beneficiary 受益人
5. the confirming bank 保兑行
6. negotiating bank 议付行
7. the accepting bank 承兑行
8. paying bank 付款行
9. the reimbursing bank 偿付行
10. With reference to... 鉴于……
11. ...under the Sales Confirmation No. SE113... 在销售确认书 SE113 号中……
12. do your utmost to... 尽力去做……
13. due to ... 由于……

⭐ *Part IV   Practical Writing Tasks*

Practice 1 Terms
Match the following business English terms and phrases with their proper Chinese meaning.

1. commercial invoice	A. 保险单
2. marine bill of lading	B. 海关发票
3. insurance policy or insurance certificate	C. 商检证
4. certificate of origin	D. 航空运单
5. inspection certificate	E. 铁路运单
6. customs invoice	F. 原产地证
7. air waybill	G. 商业发票
8. railway consignment note	H. 海运提单

Practice 2 Fill in the blank with the words and expressions given bellow. Change the form where necessary.

defer	confirm	extend	accordance	issue
punctual	accept	prompt	delete	shipment

1. The L/C should reach the Sellers one month before _____ .

2. We may accept _____ payment if the quantity is over 10,000.

3. We hope this amendment of L/C will not affect your _____ shipment of the goods.

4. We suggest you pay by bill of exchange at 30 days' documents against _____ .

5. The relative L/C should be _____ through a third bank acceptable to the seller.

6. The performance of your products must keep in exact _____ with our samples.

7. It is a great regret for us to find that there are certain clauses which don't _____ to those of the Contract.

8. In the case of sight credits, payment can be made _____ upon presentation of draft and impeccable shipping documents.

9. Please _____ the clause"by direct shipment" and insert the wording "Partial shipments and transshipment are allowed".

10. The amendment advice should reach us by March 1, failing which you must _____ the validity of the L/C to the end of May.

Practice 3 Translation

I. Translate the following sentences from Chinese into English.

1. 请即办理展证事宜，并尽早电复。

2. 通常，我方只接受保兑的、不可撤销的即期信用证。

3. 我们很遗憾地发现有些条款与合同中的条款不符。

4. 我们很遗憾地告知贵方，我们直到今天才收到你方有关上述销售确认书的信用证。

5. 烦请通知买方，我们将信用证内 C&F 纽约更改为买方负担运费。

II. Translate the following sentences from English into Chinese.

1. In spite of our numerous reminders, you haven't opened the letter of credit so far.

2. We insist on payment by irrevocable sight credit.

3. L/C at sight is what we request for all our customers.

4. We'll agree to change the terms of payment from L/C at sight to D/P at sight.

5. The expiry date of the credit being May 31, we request that you will arrange with your banker to extend it up to June 10.

Practice 4 Practical Writing
Write a letter of credit, using the following information.

> ※ You are the sales manager of ABC Company. You received the L/C from AAA Company and found several items should be amended.
>
> ※ Write a letter asking the person in charge amend the terms of payment, port of destination and the price.

★ Part V　Key Sentences for Reference

※ We suggest you to pay by bill of exchange at 30 day's documents against acceptance.

我们建议你们以 30 天期承兑交单支付。

※ Greatly satisfied with your cooperation in the past, we shall extend the relative L/C in compliance with your request for two weeks.

由于与你方过去的合作甚为满意，我方将根据你方要求，展延信用证两周。

※ It is a great pleasure to inform you that we have got all your ordered goods ready for shipment. Please establish your L/C at once.

我方有幸通知你方，我方已将你方所订货物全部备妥待运，请速开信用证。

※ After receiving our L/C, you must effect the shipment of the goods as soon as possible.

收到我方信用证以后，你方必须尽快发货。

※ Before accepting the draft, the bank will require you to produce documents such as Bills of Lading, Commercial Invoice, Packing List, etc.

在接受汇票以前，银行将要求你方出示提单、商业发票、装箱单证等。

※ We are glad to learn that you forwarded the letter of credit on May 5 to the Bank of America in San Francisco. We assume we shall receive an advice within a few days.

我们很高兴得知贵公司早于 5 月 5 日向旧金山美国银行开出信用证。我们相信日内可望收到银行通知。

※ We are glad to learn that you opened a credit with the National Bank, in favor of Smith & Co., for the amount of $100,000 covering the said order available till December 31.

我们很高兴得知贵公司对此批订货，已通过国家银行开出以史密斯公司为受益人，面额为 100,000 美元，12 月 31 日前有效的信用证。

※ We have drawn on you at 60 days' sight a draft for $90,000, under the credit No. 450 of June 6, in favor of the Tokyo Bank.

对 6 月 6 日第 450 号信用证，我公司已开出面额为 90,000 元的汇票，该汇票以东京银行为受益人，付款日期为见票后 60 天。

※ Please advise the beneficiaries that we shall amend the Credit No.1200 to read ten boxes of the articles instead of 5 boxes, otherwise unchanged.

请通知受益人，我们将第 1200 号信用证中 5 箱更改为 10 箱，其余部分不变。

※ This is solely an advice of amendment of the L/C and not constitute a Confirmation of the message.

本函仅为信用证修改通知书，并非证实书。

※ Owing to some delay on the part of our suppliers, we are not in a position to ship the goods before June 30 as stipulated in the L/C. Kindly extend the shipping date and credit validity for one month respectively.

由于供应商的延误，我们不能按信用证规定在 6 月 30 日之前发货，故请将信用证的船期和有效期分别延展 1 个月。

※ In order to pave the way for your pushing the sale of our products in your market, we will accept the payment by D/P at sight as a special accommodation.

为了你方在你市场推销我方产品铺平道路，我方将接受即期付款交单方式付款，以示特别照顾。

※ As this is the first deal between us, I hope we can trade on customary terms, i.e., Letter of credit payable against sight draft.

由于这是我们之间进行的第一笔交易，我很希望能够遵照惯例，也就是说，用即期信用证付款。

Learning Objectives

To be proficient in

➢ understanding knowledge of insurance;

➢ using key terms, useful expressions and key sentences for letters of insurance;

➢ writing a letter of insurance.

Part I   Warming-up Activities

 **Task 1**

Translate the following insurance companies into Chinese.

1. PICC Holding Company
2. PICC Property and Casualty Company Limited
3. China Life Insurance (Group) Company
4. China Life Insurance Company Limited
5. China Reinsurance (Group) Company
6. China Property Reinsurance Co., Ltd.
7. China Life Reinsurance Co., Ltd.
8. China Continent Property & Casualty Insurance Company Ltd.
9. China Insurance (Holdings) Company Limited
10. The Taiping Insurance Company, Ltd.

 **Task 2**

Read the following passage about insurance and answer the questions below.

Insurance is defined as financial protection against loss or harm. It is an arrangement by which a company gives customers financial protection against loss, damage, and delay in transit. In return, a payment known as a premium is paid by the insured to the insurance company. The insurance company agrees to pay if a specified undesirable event occurs. The result is that the burden of any loss is borne not by the unfortunate individual directly affected but by all the persons involved.

An insurer, or insurance carrier, is a company selling the insurance; the insured, or policyholder, is the person or entity buying the insurance policy. The amount of money to be charged for a certain amount of insurance coverage is called the premium.

There are many different kinds of insurance and most are rather specific and complicated. Some of the most common insurance policy options include: health insurance, sickness insurance, insurance for medical care, "major medical" insurance policy, life insurance, social insurance, personal property insurance, cargo insurance, engineering insurance, liability insurance, and investment insurance.

1. What is insurance?

2. What are the types of insurance?

⊛ *Part II   Sample Study &Writing Tips*

Sample 1 Requesting Insurance

Dear Sir / Madam,

Re: Order No. 568569

Referring to the Order No. 568569 Covering 2,000 sets of Philips Ultra-thin LCD TV,you can see that this order was placed on CFR (COST AND FREIGHT) basis.

Now we would like to have the shipment insured at you end. We will be grateful if you arrange to cover the goods on our behalf against All Risks for 120% of the invoice value.

As usual, we would like to leave the insurance arrangements to you and shall be pleased if you could have the goods covered against All Risks on our behalf for 120% of the invoice value, i.e. US$2,000.00. The premium is to be charged to us and will be paid on the presentation of the documents to our agent in San Francisco.

Looking forward to your early reply.

Yours sincerely,

Steven

🐧 Task 1

Discuss the following question: According to the above sample, what information does the letter of insurance contain?

Writing Guide

The letter of insurance generally contains information about inquiring about insurance information, asking the seller to cover insurance, discuss insurance clause, etc.

Basically, letters dealing with insurance usually are requesting insurance be taken out, making arrangements with insurance companies and discussing policy terms, explaining policies, and placing a claim with an insurance company or another responsible party.

(1) Letters of this kind usually have a reference. e.g.

Re: Policy A-3425-05

Re: Order No. 52765

The opening sentence gives reference to the previous correspondence and the purpose of the letter (about insurance). e.g.

Thank you for your letter of May 24, informing us of your insurance rate.

In response to your inquiry of the 20th of this month, we wish to quote you the rate of Marine Insurance at 0.315%, ICC (B) including War Risk on the shipment referred to in your letter.

(2) The middle part provides information of and discuss about insurance.

As to the insured value, our general practice is to insure at invoice value plus 10%.

The contract calls for an insurance policy, so a certificate of insurance will be rejected by the bank.

The rate of 0.315% is acceptable to us and we shall be glad if you will effect immediate insurance, ICC(Institute Cargo Clause) including War Risk, at the rate quoted on the goods mentioned below.

The goods will be shipped in containers, so we think it is not a must for us to insure them against the risk of breakage.

Unless you give contrary instructions, we will arrange an all-risk insurance policy for the shipment. In our opinion this type of cover is necessary for a cargo of this nature.

Your request for insurance coverage up to the inland city is acceptable on condition that such extra premium is for your account.

(3) The closing part either asks for an answer or looks forward to further communication.

We look forward to receiving the policy within the next few days. In the meantime, please confirm that you hold the goods covered.

Please let us know what particulars you need from us when we submit our claim form. We look forward to hearing from you shortly.

Sample 2 Giving Information about Insurance

Task 2

Complete the letter of giving information about insurance according to the Chinese in the parentheses.

Dear Sir / Madam,

Re: Order No. 5316

In reply to your letter of June 25, 2013 asking us to effect insurance on the above order, 1) _____（我们很高兴通知您）that we have covered the shipment with the People's Insurance Company of China against All Risks for 110% of the invoice value, i.e. $8,600.00. The policy is being prepared accordingly and the debit note for the premium will be presented to your agent in San Francisco in a week or two. For your information, 2) _____（我们现正安排由"东风号"汽船装运订单货物）which is due to sail for your port on or about July 13.

3) _____（如果有任何问题，随时联系我）.

Sincerely yours,

Linda

Sample 3 Negotiating Insurance Policies

Task 3

Compose a letter of negotiation for insurance policies by using the given statements.

1. Please advise us as soon as possible
2. We have received your letter of May 27 in regard to insurance
3. Normally we cover insurance WPA (水渍险) and WAR Risk in the absence of definite instructions from our customers
4. and the extra premium will again be borne by the buyer

> Dear Ms.Linda,
>
> Re: Order No. NC-329
>   Order No. Mc-471
>
>   1) _____ . Now we would like to inform you of the following:
>   2) _____ . If you desire to cover All Risks, we can provide such coverage at a slightly higher premium. As to the insured value, our general practice is to insure at invoice value plus 10%. Any additional premium for insurance coverage of 110% of the invoice, if so required, shall be charged to buyer's account.
>   Risks other than All risks and War Risk can be covered here, 3) _____ .
>   We hope this information is helpful. 4) _____ if you wish us to change the insurance coverage on this order.
>
>   Faithfully yours,
>   Susan

Sample 4 Cancel a Renter's Insurance Policy

Task 4

Read the following letter of canceling a renter's insurance and insert the imaginative unknown information.

> The Date
> Policy Number: ✕✕✕✕✕✕✕✕✕
> Fax Number: ✕✕✕-✕✕✕-✕✕✕✕
> Alternative Fax Number: ✕✕✕-✕✕✕-✕✕✕✕
>
> [Your insurance provider]
> Their street address,
> Their apt. number,
> Their City, State Zip code

To [Your insurance provider],

I will no longer need a renter's insurance policy for the location of: Your street address, Apt. number, City, State Zip code. I recently graduated, and I am no longer living at the location. I would appreciate it if [Your insurance provider] could cancel my renter's insurance policy as soon as possible. Thank you and have a great day.

Sincerely,

Your name

Your signature

Document should include: Date, your address, your policy number, their address, fax number, time of cancellation, and the reason for stopping the policy.

Document does not need: Any new addresses or contact information.

Sample 5 Complaint Letter to State Insurance Commission

 **Task 5**

Read the following complaint letter to State Insurance Commission and insert the imaginative unknown information.

Name of State Insurance Commission
Street Address
City, State, Zip Code

Dear Insurance Commissioner:

I have filed the attached insurance claim with _____ (insert name of your insurance company) on _____ (insert date of claim). My physician has deemed this therapy medically necessary for my medical condition, but my insurance company has denied me access to the standard of care. I have had the following specific problems with this insurance company:

(List all of your problems such as refusal to cover physician prescribed therapy, claim has not been paid or denied, etc.)

Please accept this letter as a formal written complaint against _____ (insert name of your insurance company).

Sincerely,
Your Name
Your Address, City, State, Zip Code, and Telephone Number
cc: Medical Director, _____ (insert name of your insurance company).
Your Physician

✈ *Part III　Vocabulary in Use*

insurance /ɪnˈʃuərəns/	*n.*	(contract made by a company or society, or by the state, to provide a) guarantee of compensation for loss, damage, sickness, death, etc. in return for regular payment 保险（契约）
casualty /ˈkæʒuəlti/	*n.*	person who is killed or injured in war or in an accident （战争或事故中的）伤亡者
property /ˈprɔpəti/	*n.*	thing or things owned; possession (s) 所有物；财产；资产
transit /ˈtrænsit/	*n.*	the process of being moved or carried from one place to another 运输，运送
premium /ˈpriːmɪəm/	*n.*	an amount of money that you pay once or regularly for an insurance policy 保险费
specify /ˈspesɪfaɪ/	*v.*	state sth, especially by giving an exact measurement, time, exact instructions, etc. 规定，指定，确定；详细说明，具体说明
individual /ˌɪndɪˈvɪdʒuəl/	*n.*	A single human being considered apart from a society or community 个体
entity /ˈentɪti/	*n.*	something that exists as a single and complete unit 实体
invoice /ˈɪnvɔɪs/	*n.*	list of goods sold or services provided with the price(s) charged, esp. sent as a bill 发票；发货清单；服务费用清单
container /kənˈteɪnə/	*n.*	a box, bottle, etc. in which sth can be stored or transported 容器；集装箱
breakage /ˈbreɪkɪdʒ/	*n.*	an object that has been broken 破损
cover /ˈkʌvə/	*v.*	insure sb/sth against loss, etc. 给某人或某事物保险
cargo /ˈkɑːgəu/	*n.*	the goods carried in a ship or plane 货物
document /ˈdɔkjumənt/	*n.*	an official paper or book that gives information about sth, or that can be used as evidence or proof of sth 文件；证书
coverage /ˈkʌvərɪdʒ/	*n.*	inclusion in an insurance policy or protective plan 保险项目
physician /fɪˈzɪʃn/	*n.*	a doctor, especially one who is a specialist in general medicine and not surgery 医生；内科医生
prescribe /prɪˈskraɪb/	*v.*	(of a doctor) to tell sb to take a particular medicine or have a particular treatment 开药；开处方
therapy /ˈθerəpi/	*n.*	treatment of illness or disability 治疗

Expressions

1. the insured, or policyholder 被保险人；投保人
2. an insurer, or insurance carrier 保险公司
3. insurance policy 保险证书；保险单
4. insurance coverage 保险项目；保险覆盖面；保险范围
5. take out insurance 买保险；投保

6. ICC (Institute Cargo Clause) 协会货物条款

7. Philips Ultra-thin LCD TV 飞利浦超薄液晶电视机

8. CFR (COST AND FREIGHT) 成本加运费

9. be paid on the presentation of the documents 以提交单据为支付条件

10. debit note 欠款单，借记单

11. WPA (With Particular Average) 单独海损赔债，担保单独海损，水渍险

Part IV   Practical Writing Tasks

Practice 1Terms
Match the following business English terms and phrases with their proper Chinese meaning.

1. insurance coverage	A. 中国保险条款
2. Special Additional Risk	B. 保险费
3. insurance agent	C. 保险额
4. insurance policy	D. 特别附加险
5. Institute Cargo Clauses	E. 保险凭证
6. insurance certificate	F. 保险代理人
7. China Insurance Clauses	G. 保单
8. insurance claim	H. 协会货物条款
9. insurance premium	I. 保险索赔
10. insurance amount	J. 保险范围

Practice 2 Fill in the blank with the words and expressions given bellow. Change the form where necessary.

insurance policy	coverage	cover	approval	contact
terms and conditions	shipping advice	claim	response	insure

1. We are writing to enquire about the _____ which you can provide.

2. We appreciate your sending us your present _____ at your earliest convenience.

3. This is an insurance policy with extensive _____ .

4. We sincerely hope that our request will meet with your _____ .

5. We have _____ the above shipment against All Risks.

6. We are looking forward to your prompt _____ .

7. Please send us your _____ as soon as possible.

8. If you demand to _____ against other additional risks, the extra premium involved will be for buyer's account.

9. Please _____ the PICC on your side for further particulars.

10. If any damage to the goods occurs, a _____ may be filed with the insurance agent of PICC at your end, who will undertake to compensate you for the loss sustained.

Practice 3 Translation

I. Translate the following sentences from Chinese into English.

1. 很高兴收到您要求我方对贵方货物投保的来函。

2. 这是一项承保范围广泛的保险。

3. 对于 CIF 交易，我们一般按发票金额的 110% 投保风险。

4. 我们已按发票金额 110% 投保。

5. 如有需要，投保额外险别的额外保险费需由买方承担。

II. Translate the following sentences from English into Chinese.

1. Prior to shipment, we want to make sure whether your company makes insurance for the goods to be delivered to us.

2. We are in great pleasure to receive the notification that you want us to charge the insurance in transportation of a group of statues, from Shanghai to London.

3. According to your letter of October 16 enquiring for insurance, we have insure your goods to Ping An Insurance Company of China, Ltd. against All Risks.

4. We know that according to your usual practice, you insure that goods only for 10% above invoice value; therefore the extra premium will be for our account.

5. As our usual practice, insurance covers basic risks only, at 110% of the invoice value.

Practice 4 Practical Writing

Write a letter, using the following information.

※ You are an employee of an insurance company. Your customer has written to request you to insure the goods (Order No. 123 for 5,000 Cartons of Silk Blouses) for an amount of 120% of invoice value.

※ Write a letter of 120-140 words to the customer, informing the customer of your usual practice to take out insurance for 110% of invoice value and the extra premium will be for the customer's account.

Part V Key Sentences for Reference

※ Please insure us the following goods against all risks.

请将我方以下货物投保综合险。

※ The underwriters are responsible for the claim as far as it is within the scope of cover.

只要是在保险责任范围内，保险公司就应负责赔偿。

※ Generally speaking, we insure W.P.A on CIF sales.

一般来讲，以 CIF 成交的话我们投保水渍险。

※ The extent of insurance is stipulated in the basic policy form and in the various risk clause.

保险的范围写在基本保险单和各种险别的条款里。

※ What risks is the People's Insurance Company of China able to cover?

中国人民保险公司承保的险别有哪些？

※ This is an insurance policy with extensive coverage.

这是一项承保范围广泛的保险。

※ What kind of insurance are you able to provide for my consignment?

贵公司能为我的这批货保哪些险呢？

※ What's the insurance premium?

保险费是多少？

※ The cover paid for will vary according to the type of goods and the circumstances.

保险费用按照货物类别的具体情况会有所不同。

※ According to co-insurance clauses, the insured person must pay usually 20 percent of the total expenses covered.

根据共同保险条款，保险人通常必须付全部费用的 20%。

※ The insurance rate for such kink of risk will vary according to the kind.

这类险别的保险费率将根据货物种类而定。

※ The total premium is 800 U.S. dollars.

保险费总共是 800 美元。

※ I'll have the goods covered against Free from Particular Average.

我将为货物投保平安险。

※ Please insure the shipment for RMB 5000 against All Risks.

请将这批货物投保综合险人民币 5000 元。

※ We've cover insurance on these goods for 10% above the invoice value against All Risks.

我们已经将这些货物按发票金额加 10% 投保综合险。

※ Generally speaking, aviation insurance is much cheaper than marine insurance.

空运保险一般要比海运保险便宜。

※ Are there any other clauses in marine policies?

海运险还包括其他条款吗?

※ As our usual practice, insurance covers basic risks only, at 110 percent of the invoice value. If coverage against other risks is required, such as breakage, leakage, TPND, hook and contamination damages, the extra premium involved would be for the buyer's account.

按照我们的惯例,只保基本险,按发票金额 110% 投保。如果要加保其他险别,例如破碎险、渗漏险、盗窃遗失险、钩损和污染险等,额外保险费由买方负担。

※ We can serve you with a broad range of coverage against all kinks of risks for sea transport.

我公司可以承保海洋运输的所有险别。

※ Please tell me whether I need to purchase a foreign student policy.

请告诉我,我是否需要购买外国学生保险。

※ I'd like to know whether basic health insurance coverage should include benefits for outpatient, hospital, surgery and medical expenses.

我想知道基本健康保险所列的项目是否应包括医院门诊、住院、手术及药品等费用的赔偿。

Inquiry,Offer & Counter-offer

Learning Objectives

To be proficient in

➤ understanding knowledge of inquiry, offer & counter-offer in business negotiation;

➤ using key terms, useful expressions and key sentences for letters of inquiry, offer & counter-offer;

➤ writing a letter of inquiry, offer & counter-offer.

Part I Warming-up Activities

 Task 1

Answer the question: How do you bargain before you decide to buy something? In business negotiations there are four key links, what are they?

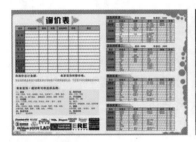  

Task 2

Read the following passage about Inquiry, Offer & Counter-offer and answer the questions below according to what you have read:

In business negotiations there are four key links: inquiry, offer, counter-offer and acceptance.

Inquiry is the first step in business negotiations to seek a supply of products, service or information. In the international business the importer may send an inquiry to an exporter, inviting a quotation and/or an offer for the goods he wishes to buy or simply asking for some general information about these goods.

Generally speaking, inquiries fall into two categories: a General Inquiry and a Specific Inquiry.In a General Inquiry, the importer may ask only for catalogues, price lists, samples, or quotations, etc., in order to get a general idea of the business scope of the exporter. In a Specific Inquiry, the importer points out what products he needs and asks for a quotation or an offer for this item.

A quotation is a reply to an enquiry, giving information about the goods enquired. It is also a promise without engagement to supply the goods on certain terms.

An offer is a reply to an enquiry usually made by the seller, giving relative information about the goods. It is a promise to supply goods on the stated terms and conditions. It usually contains all necessary terms of business for the buyer's consideration and acceptance.

A firm offer is made when sellers promise to sell goods at a stated price within a stated period of time. A firm offer must be clear, complete and definite, and the validity must be clearly stated.

A non-firm offer is usually indicated by means of sending catalogues, price lists and quotations.

If a buyer does not agree with any or some of the transaction terms of a quotation or a firm offer,he will state his own terms and conditions to renew the received quotation or offer. This renewed offer is called counter-offer.

A counter-offer is a partial rejection of the original offer and a counter proposal by the buyer for the amendment of certain unacceptable terms.

1. What are the four key links in business negotiations?

2. What are the two types of inquiries?

3. What are the difference between a firm offer and a non-firm offer?

4. What is counter-offer?

⭐ Part II   Sample Study &Writing Tips

Sample 1 Inquiry

> Dear Sirs,
>
>   On the recommendation of Osaka Chamber of Commerce and Industry, we have learned that you are manufacturers of Ladies' and Men's Sports Wear. Now we are particularly interested in importing various range of Ladies' and Men's Sports Wear.
>
>   If your products are of good quality, and we receive a favorable offer, we may be able to place a large order with you. With this mind, we think it would also be helpful if you can furnish us some illustrated catalogues together with your lowest quotation.
>
>   As to our credit standing, please refer to The Bank of Beijing, China.
>
>   Your early reply will be highly appreciated.
>
> Yours faithfully,
>
> Thomas

🐧 Task 1

Discuss the following question: According to the above sample, what aspects should one take into consideration when writing a letter of inquiry and a reply to an inquiry?

Writing Tips: Enquiries & Replies to Inquiries

    Inquiries may be made nowadays by postal letters, faxes or emails. When making an inquiry, one should take the following aspects into consideration.

1) At the beginning of the letter, tell the receiver where you learnt of his company and its products. Moreover, you can introduce your own business and the products it deals in.

2) You should state simply, clearly and concisely what you want—general information, a catalogue, price list, or a sample and ask for a quotation or an offer for the item.

3) Enquiry should be specific and provide the necessary details to enable the receiver to answer the questions completely. Describe the commodities or service of your interest as specifically as possible and tell the receiver the name of the commodity or service which you inquire for and its specifications, quality, available quantity, price, way of delivery, date of shipment, terms of payment, etc.

4) Introduce briefly your market situation and emphasize your desire for the reasonable and competitive prices which they will offer.

5) State the possibility of your making order for drawing their interest and attention and request an early reply.

A typical reply to an inquiry usually consists of the following aspects:

1) Express thanks for the customer's interest in your products or service and confirm that you can or cannot help.

2) Give a full answer to the enquiry and explain how it is suitable for your customer's needs.

3) State that you are sending a catalogue, a quotation or even make an offer.

4) Explain how the customer can get hand-on experience of the product:

> offer to send samples or get reply to visit with samples / demo;

> state the location of distributor's showroom near the inquirer's address;

> announce an exhibit at a forthcoming trade fair.

5) End the letter by hoping for business and supply further information if required.

6) Try to explain the reason politely if you cannot do as requested and have to decline an inquiry.

Sample 2 An Offer

Dear Sirs,

Thank you for your inquiry of March 22 of your interest in our cotton piece goods.

We are in a position to supply products in various design and colors. We take pleasure in making you an offer as follows:

Price: US$ 3 per yard FOB Guangzhou

Payment: by irrevocable confirmed sight L/C

Shipment:1 month after order confirmed

Validity: one week from the date quoted

Looking forward to receiving your order early.

Sincerely yours,

Zhaqng Huan

Sales Manager

Task 2

Discuss the following question: According to the above sample, what contents does an offer letter generally consist of?

Tips for Making an Offer

An offer letter generally consists of the following contents:

1) An expression of sincere thanks for the enquiry.

2) Details of the offer and trade terms, including:

> name of commodity, quality or specifications;

> quantity;

> unit price and price terms, discounts, commission and their conditions;

> terms of payment, package and date of delivery / shipment.

3) Firm offer: the period for which the offer is valid.

4) Non-firm offer: a remark to the effect that the offer is without engagement.

5) Favorable comments on the goods themselves, if appropriate.

6) An expression of hope that the offer will be accepted and hope for a prompt reply.

Sample 3 A Non-firm Offer

 **Task 3**

Complete the letter of a non-firm offer according to the Chinese in the parentheses.

> Dear Sirs,
>
> Your letter of April 16 asking us to offer you the embroidered dress has received our immediate attention. We are pleased to be told that 1) _____ (我们的产品销路很好).
>
> 2) _____ (按照你们的要求) , we are making you the following special offer subject to market fluctuations.
>
> Price: at US$50 each piece CIF London
>
> Payment: By irrevocable L/C, payable by draft at sight.
>
> 3) _____ (如果你们觉得这个报价可以接受) , let us have your reply as soon as possible.
>
> Sincerely yours,
>
> Susan

Sample 4 A Firm Offer for Color TV Sets

 **Task 4**

Compose a letter of a firm offer for color TV sets with the given information.

1. Payment

2. Shipment

3. Price

4. Quality

5. Quantity

6. Commodity

> Dear Sirs,
>
> We acknowledge receipt of your letter dated August 18, from which we note that you wish to have an offer from us for 2,000 color TV sets, for shipment to Sydney.

In reply, we are making you, subject to your reply reaching us by August 25, the following offer:

1) _____ : Rainbow brand Color TV sets, 29 inches
2) _____ : 2,000 sets
3) _____ : As per attached specification sheets
4) _____ : at US$799 per set CIF C2% Sydney
5) _____ : During August / September
6) _____ : By confirmed, irrevocable L/C payable by draft at sight

Our color TV sets are of top quality and reasonable price. They give users a clear and stable picture, natural vivid color and sweet sound. We can also provide spare components and after-sales service to the customers. All our color TV sets are guaranteed for one year.

This offer is valid for 10 days. As we are able to offer prompt delivery, we hope to receive your email order in the near future.

Faithfully yours,

Susan

Sample 5 A Letter of Counter-offer on Payment Terms

Dear Sirs,

Thank you for your quotation of July 15 for 1,000 sets Panasonic TH-L32C5C Color TV. We find your price as well as delivery date satisfactory, however we would give our suggestion of an alteration of your payment terms.

Our past purchase of other household electricalappliances from you has been paid as a rule by confirmed, irrevocable letter of credit at sight. On this basis, it has indeed cost us a great deal.

In view of our long business relations and our amicable cooperation prospects, we suggest that you accept"Cash against Documents on arrival of goods".

It is hoped that you will consider our counter-offer most favorably and inform us of your early acceptance of our counter-offer.

Yours faithfully,

Jackie

🐧 Task 5

Discuss the following question: According to the above sample, what contents does a counter-offer letter generally consist of?

Tips for Making a Counter-offer

When making a counter offer one should state the terms explicitly and use words very carefully so as to avoid ambiguity or misunderstanding.

A counter-offer letter generally consists of the following contents:

1) Express sincere thanks for the offer;

2) Express regret for being unable to accept the offer;

3) State the reason for the non-acceptance;

4) Give advice on how to conclude a business and make suggestion for modifying the terms and conditions upon which you disagree;

5) Urge the offeree to accept the counter-offer and express wish for future cooperation.

⭐ Part III   Vocabulary in Use

quotation /kwəu'teɪʃən/	*n.*	a written statement of exactly how much money something will cost 报价；报价单
counter-offer /'kauntərɔfə/	*n.*	offer made in response to 还价
transaction /træn'zækʃne/	*n.*	a business deal or action, such as buying or selling something 交易
amendment /ə'mendmənt/	*n.*	a small change or improvement that is made to a law or a document 修改；修订
reasonable /'ri:zənəbəl/	*adj.*	(of prices) not too expensive, acceptable （指价格）不太贵的，可接受的
competitive /kəm'petɪtɪv/	*adj.*	(of products or prices) cheaper than others but still of good quality （指产品或价格）富有竞争力的
specification /ˌspesɪfɪ'keɪʃən/	*n.*	details and instructions describing the design, materials, etc. of something to be made or done 规格；规格说明
commission /kə'mɪʃən/	*n.*	payment to someone for selling goods which increases with the quantity of goods sold 佣金；回扣；酬劳金
ambiguity /ˌæmbɪ'gju:iti/	*n.*	presence of more than one meaning 不止一种意思；歧义
chamber /'tʃeɪmbə/	*n.*	a hall in a public building that is used for formal meetings 会所
standing /'stændɪŋ/	*adj.*	the position or reputation of someone/something within a group of people or in an organization 名望；身份
embroider /ɪm'brɔɪdə/	*v.*	decorate cloth by sewing a pattern, picture, or words on it with coloured threads 刺绣；绣花
compliance /kəm'plaɪəns/	*n.*	the practice of obeying rules or requests made by people in authority 依从；顺从
fluctuation /ˌflʌktʃu'eɪʃən/	*n.*	a change in a price, amount, level etc. 涨落；波动
acknowledge /ək'nɔlɪdʒ/	*v.*	tell someone that you have received something that they sent to you 告知收到
confirm /kən'fə:m/	*v.*	make valid or binding by a formal or legal act 批准；认可；确认

| irrevocable /ɪ'revəkəbəl/ | *adj.* | that cannot be changed; final 不能变更的；不能撤销的 |
| draft /drɑ:ft / | *n.* | a written order for money to be paid by a bank, especially from one bank to another 汇票 |

Expressions

1. General Inquiry 一般询价

2. Specific Inquiry 具体询价

3. a promise without engagement 没有约束力的承诺

4. a firm offer 实盘

5. a non-firm offer 虚盘

6. a counter-offer 还盘

7. take … into consideration 考虑；考虑到

8. consist of 由……组成

9. terms of payment 付款条件；支付条款

10. conclude a business 达成贸易；成交生意

11. modify the terms and conditions 修改条款

12. Osaka Chamber of Commerce and Industry 大阪工商商会

13. Ladies' and Men's Sports Wear 男女运动服装

14. CIF: (commerce 商业、贸易术语) cost, insurance, freight (included in the price) 到岸价（包括成本、保险费、运费）

15. irrevocable L/C 不可撤销信用证

16. payable by draft at sight 见票即付

17. acknowledge receipt of 确认已收到

18. Rainbow brand Color TV sets, 29 inches 29 英寸长虹牌彩电

19. CIF C2% Sydney 悉尼到岸价，2% 佣金

20. spare components 备用部件

21. after-sales service 售后服务

22. cotton piece goods 布匹

23. be in a position to do: be able to do something because you have the ability, money, or power to do it（因为有能力、金钱或权力而）能够做某事

24. Panasonic TH-L32C5C Color TV 松下 TH- L32C5C 液晶彩电

25. confirmed, irrevocable letter of credit at sight 保兑的、不可撤销的即期信用证

26. in view of 考虑到；鉴于

27. cash against documents on arrival of goods 货到后凭单付款

⭐ *Part IV   Practical Writing Tasks*

Practice 1 Terms
Match the following business English terms and phrases with their proper Chinese meaning.

1. negotiate the price　　　　　　　　　　　　　A. 成交

2. push sales	B. 实盘
3. conclude the business	C. 交货
4. adjust the price	D. 推销
5. place a trial order	E. 不可撤销信用证
6. make delivery	F. 议价
7. terms of payment	G. 见票即付
8. a firm offer	H. 试下订单
9. irrevocable L/C	I. 支付条款
10. payable by draft at sight	J. 调整价格

Practice 2 Fill in the blank with the words and expressions given bellow. Change the form where necessary.

reasonable	enquire	credit	discount	offer
payment	quotation	quote	confirmation	order

1. We are writing to _____ about the current price of high quality gloves.

2. If your price is _____ , we may place a large order with you.

3. As to terms of _____ , we require L/C.

4. We give a 10% _____ for cash payment.

5. As for terms of payment, it is our custom to trade on the basis of a confirmed and irrevocable letter of _____ .

6. If your _____ is competitive, we are ready to conduct substantial business with you.

7. We will _____ you the lowest price if you send us your specific enquiry.

8. We are confident that our quotation will be acceptable to you and await your initial _____ .

9. We regret to inform that we cannot accept your _____ , because your prices are much higher than those of your competitors.

10. As requested, we are offering you the following goods subjected to our final _____ .

Practice 3 Translation

I. Translate the following sentences from Chinese into English.

1. 如果你方报价有竞争力，装运期可接受，我们将大量订购。

2. 此报盘 15 天内有效。

3. 我们可以按国际市场价格给您报价。

4. 我们很难说服客户以这个价格购买你方产品。

5. 与国际市场价格相比，我们的价格是合理的。

II. Translate the following sentences from English into Chinese.

1. We ask you kindly deliver us as soon as possible your latest price list of your computers with the lowest quotations, together with an illustrated catalogue.

2. If your quality is good and the price is suitable for our market, we would consider signing a long-term contract with you.

3. As we are likely to place large orders regularly we trust you will consider the allowance of some special concessions.

4. The quality of our product is good and the price is reasonable so we are confident that you will accept our offer dated June 16.

5. If we had not thought of our long term business relationship, we wouldn't have made you a firm offer at this price.

Practice 4 Practical Writing
Write letters, using the following information.

A Letter of Inquiry

询价信 (Letter 1)

1. 发信人：Mr. David Johnson

2. 收信人：Mr. Peter Kevil

3. 发信日期：2013 年 12 月 30 日

4. 内容：Mr. David Johnson 欲购买 Mr. Peter Kevil 所在的 HP 公司生产的激光打印机 (jet printer)，写信了解有关价格以及售后服务的情况。

A Letter of Reply

报价信 (Letter 2)

1. 发信人：Mr. Peter Kevil

2. 收信人：Mr. David Johnson

3. 发信日期：2014 年 1 月 2 日

4. 内容：Mr. Peter Kevil 非常感谢 Mr. David Johnson 对他们公司生产的激光打印机感兴趣，随信附上目录以及价目表，并告知 HP 公司为客户提供优良的服务。不仅如此，如果购买的数量较大，还可以享受折扣。

_____

_____

_____

_____

_____

_____

_____

_____

⭐ Part V   Key Sentences for Reference

※ We are in the market for Chinese hand-made art crafts and we would appreciate you letting us know your best possible quotation, indicating origin, detailed specification, packing, quantity available.

我们想购买中国的手工艺品，若你们能向我方报最优惠的价格，说明产地、具体规格、包装以及可供数量，我们将不胜感激。

※ Please let us have your best quotation by tomorrow together with the appropriate time of shipment.

请于明天告知我方贵方最优惠的报价和装船日期。

※ If your prices are competitive, we can probably let you have regular orders.

如果贵公司价格有竞争力，我方也许会经常向贵公司订购。

※ We thank you for your inquiry of May 16, and can offer you the following items. This offer will remain open until the receipt of your email by return.

感谢贵方 5 月 16 日询盘，现就如下货物向你们报盘，此报盘有效期至收到贵方邮件回复。

※ As requested, we are enclosing our quotation in triplicate and shall appreciate your placing the order with us as early as possible.

应按贵方要求，特此随函附寄我方报价单一式三份，如蒙早日购货将不胜感激。

※ We have much pleasure in enclosing a quotation sheet for our products and trust that their high quality will induce you to place a trial order.

非常高兴寄上我们的产品报价单，我们相信我们产品的质量会促使你们试下订单。

※ As requested, we are offering you the following goods subjected to our final confirmation.

根据要求，我方现就以下货物向贵方报价，该报价以我方最后确认为准。

※ We believe that the price we offer you can compete well with those of other firms.

我们相信我们给你们的报价与其他公司相比更具竞争力。

※ We'll place a substantial order with you if your price is reasonable.

如果你方的价格合理，我们将大量订货。

※ In order to conclude the business, we may make some concessions.

为了成交，我们可以做些让步。

※ Compared with what is quoted by other supplier, your price is uncompetitive.

与其他供应商报价相比，你方价格缺乏竞争力。

※ Our counter offer is well in line with the international market, fair and reasonable.

我方还盘与国际市场相符，公平合理。

※ Your counter offer is much too low, especially considering the small amount of your order.

你的还盘太低，尤其是这么小的订单量。

※ This is our rock bottom price, we can't make any concessions.

这是我们的底价，我们不能再做任何让步。

※ If you double the order, we may consider giving you an 8% discount.

如果订单翻倍的话，我们可以考虑给你 8% 的折扣。

※ We should book a trial order with you provided you will give us 5% commission.

如果你能给我 5% 佣金的话，我们可以先下个试单。

※ In view of our good cooperation over the past few years, we prepare to accept your price.

鉴于过去几年的良好合作，我们准备接受你方的价格。

Letter of
Application for a Position

Learning Objectives

To be proficient in

- understanding knowledge of job application;
- using key terms, useful expressions and key sentences for letters of application for a position;
- writing a letter of application for a position.

Part I Warming-up Activities

Task 1

Work in pairs or small groups to list as many jobs as you can. Put the jobs in order of your preference and give your reasons.

For example: teacher, doctor, engineer, cashier, lawyer, etc.

Task 2

Work in pairs and discuss how to make your job interview successful.

Task 3

Read the following passage about a job application letter and answer the following question: What are the main contents of a job application?

It's everybody's dream to find an ideal job. But how? Facing the fierce competition in the job market, a graduate should get well prepared for everything during the job hunting. An effective job application letter, a satisfactory résumé and an appropriate interview are the first things to pay attention to.

A job application letter is a short and introductory business letter written for the purpose of getting a job. In the letter, the applicant needs to identify the job or position he wants, clarify his qualifications, and request for an interview.

Letters of application are usually characterized by formality, like other business letters. Therefore, it should be written formally and briefly in the most common. It's similar to a business letter.

In general, as an applicant, you need first to explain your origin of the news, your qualification of the application, and briefly state your education, work experience, works, theses and subjects you studied or plan to study. Finally, you should give your reasons for which you choose this position.

You can, according to what is required, provide your resume, graduation certificate (diploma), or certificate of degree in study, recommendatory letters and other necessary materials. You may talk about your work plan or aim in your letter.

Part II Sample Study &Writing Tips

Sample 1 Application for Position of Secretary

P. O. Box No. 1123
London, England
January 27, 2014

Richard Thomas Baldwin LTD.
151 Gower Street
London, England

Dear Sir/Madam:

Re: Application for Position of Secretary

In answer to your ad. in today's "Daily Mirror" for a secretary, I'd like to apply for the post. The job is attractive to me. I love it and I'm good at it.

My qualifications are as follows :

I'm 22, born in London. I graduated from London Commercial College in 1991, majoring in Foreign Trade. I've got three-year experiences as a private secretary to Mr. Evans Smith, General manager of the Universal Trading Company with salary $3000 per month. I feel quite qualified for the post in your office. I'm a sociable girl with active character in nature.

If these meet your requirements, please grant me an interview. Thank you in advance of your early reply.

Encl: A copy of my Diploma

A copy of my Resume

A copy of my I.D. Card

Yours sincerely,

Edward Murry

🐧 Task 1

Discuss the format of an application letter according to the above sample.

 # Sample 2 Application for the position of senior receptionist

🐧 Task 2

Complete the letter of application for the position of senior receptionist according to the Chinese in the parentheses.

18 Wuyi Avenue

Changsha

26th January, 2014

The Personnel Director,

Beijing Hotel,

Beijing 33 East Chang'an Street (Dong Chang'an Jie)

Dear Sir/Madam,

1) _____ (我写信想申请高级接待员的 职位)as advertised in this months' *Hotel Review*.

I am a fully trained receptionist with a diploma in Leisure and Tourism Studies, and 2) _____ (我有三年的工作经验). I currently work as a receptionist at the Alex Hua Tian Hotel in Changsha.

I would like to apply for the position advertised as I feel I have the necessary experience for the job. 3) _____ (我有良好的计算机技能). I am sociable and well organized, and I enjoy working with people.

I enclose a copy of my CV and a completed application form. 4) _____ _____(我期待着您的回音).

Yours sincerely,

Rose Smith

Sample 3 Application for the Position of Advertising Designer

January 27, 2014

Ms.Jiang Haiyan

Shanghai Rongsheng Advertisement Co. Ltd.

Dear Ms. Chen,

I would like to apply for the position of Advertising Designer of your honorable company advertised in yesterday's *China Daily*. In the past few years, I have engaged myself in full-time design activities, with quite a few design works which are popular with the clients. With my studies and work experiences, I'm confident that I'm completely qualified for the position.

One of the reasons that I intend to work in your company is that you have been the pioneer in the advertising industry for the past years and created a great number of excellent works of design. If I can become a member of your creative group, I will greatly improve my career development in the future. Of course I can also make the greatest contribution for your company.

You will find enclosed a photocopy of my ID card, a photocopy of my university diploma, and a photocopy of my technical qualification certificate.

If my application has convinced you of my ability to satisfy you, I should welcome the opportunity to talk with you, so that you may judge my personal qualifications further.

Sincerely yours,

Jordan Lee

Task 3

Discuss the following question: According to the above three samples, what aspects should one take into consideration when writing an application letter?

The Standard Parts of an Application Letter

1) Opening Paragraph

Briefly identify yourself and the position you are applying for. Add how you found out about the vacancy.

2) Paragraph 2

Give the reasons why you are interested in working for the company and why you wish to be considered for that particular post. State you relevant qualifications and experience, as well as your personal qualities that makes a suitable candidate.

3) Paragraph 3

Inform them that you have enclosed your current CV and add any further information that you think could help your case.

4) Closing Paragraph

Give your availability for interview, thank them for their consideration, restate your interest and close the letter.

Sample 4 Application for the Position of Senior Clerk

 **Task 4**

Compose a letter of application for the position of senior clerk by using the given statements.

1. I believe that my education and experience will prove useful for work in your office

2. I graduated from the English Language Department of Beijing Foreign Studies University

3. In reply to your advertisement in today's newspaper regarding a vacancy in your office

4. you will give me a personal interview at your convenience

> Dear Sir,
>
> 　　1) ＿＿＿＿＿＿＿＿＿＿ , I wish to apply for the position of senior clerk, which you have specified.
>
> 　　I feel confident that I can meet your special requirements indicating that the candidate must have a high command of English, for 2) ＿＿＿＿＿＿＿＿＿ two years ago.
>
> 　　In addition to my study of English while in the University, I have worked for three years as a secretary in the firm of ABC Trading Co. Ltd.
>
> 　　The main reason for changing my employment is to gain more experience with a superior trading company like yours. 3) ＿＿＿＿＿＿＿＿＿＿＿ .
>
> 　　I am enclosing my personal history, certificate of graduation and letter of recommendation from the president of the University. I shall be obliged if 4) ＿＿＿＿＿＿ .
>
> 　　　　　　　　　　　　　　　　　　　　　　　Very truly yours,
>
> 　　　　　　　　　　　　　　　　　　　　　　　Teresa

Sample 5 Application for a Network Maintenance Engineer

January 27, 2014

P.O. Box27

Central University for Nationalities

Beijing, China 100081

Dear Sir/Madam:

Your advertisement for a Network Maintenance Engineer in the January 20th, 2014 *Beijing Daily* interested me because the position that you described sounds exactly like the kind of job I am seeking.

According to the advertisement, your position requires top university, Bachelor or above in Computer Science or equivalent field and proficient in Windows 8.1 Operating System. I feel that I am competent to meet the requirements. I will be graduating from Graduate School of Tsinghua University this year with a M.S. degree. My studies have included courses in computer control and management.

During my education, I have grasped the principals of my major and skills of practice. Not only have I passed CET-6, but more importantly I can communicate with others freely in English. My ability to write and speak English is out of question.

I would appreciate your time in reviewing my enclosed resume and if there is any additional information you require, please contact me. I would welcome an opportunity to meet with you for a personal interview.

Sincerely,

Li Hong

Task 5

Discuss the following question: According to the above five samples, how should one write an application letter?

Writing Tips for an Effective Application Letter

How to write an effective application letter

1. Specifically state what it is that you are applying for or interested in applying for (e.g., the position, appointment, student or other visa, extension on a deadline, loan, credit card, etc.).

2. Identify the reason that you are applying. Be as specific as possible.

3. Give the reasons that you feel you merit or qualify for the position or object/thing you are applying for, if applicable (e.g., your goals, experience, qualifications or accomplishments, positive traits, and so forth).

4. Identify what you hope to accomplish by sending your letter and the action you would like the recipient to take.

5. Indicate the date by which you would like a response to your letter or by which you would like the action to be taken.

6. Refer to any other documents you have included with your letter, such as application or other forms, letters of recommendation, resume, examples of your work, etc.

7. Include a request for any information you would like to be sent, if applicable.

8. Include your contact information, such as e-mail address or phone number where you can most easily be reached and the time(s) when you available for calls, etc.

9. Close your letter by sincerely thanking the person for his/her time or for any assistance he/she can give you.

⊛ *Part III   Vocabulary in Use*

application /ˌæplɪ'keɪʃən/	*n.*	a formal (often written) request for sth, such as a job, permission to do sth or a place at a college or university 申请
fierce /fɪəs/	*adj.*	done with a lot of energy and strong feelings 激烈的
applicant /'æplɪkənt/	*n.*	a person who makes a formal request for sth (= applies for it), especially for a job, a place at a college or university, etc. 申请人；求职者
clarify /'klærɪfaɪ/	*v.*	make sth clearer or easier to understand 使明晰；详细阐明
qualification /ˌkwɔlɪfɪ'keɪʃən/	*n.*	a skill or type of experience that you need for a particular job or activity （任职）资格；条件
formality /fɔ:'mælɪti/	*n.*	something that you must do as a formal or official part of an activity or process 规范；正统
thesis /'θi:sɪs/	*n.*	a long piece of writing completed by a student as part of a university degree, based on their own research 论题；论文
certificate /sə'tɪfɪkət/	*n.*	an official document proving that you have completed a course of study or passed an exam; a qualification obtained after a course of study or an exam 证明；证书
diploma /dɪ'pləumə/	*n.*	a document showing that you have completed a course of study or part of your education 毕业文凭；毕业证书
honorable /'ɔnərəbəl/	*adj.*	deserving or winning honor and respect 值得尊敬的
equivalent /ɪ'kwɪvələnt/	*adj.*	equal in value, amount, meaning, importance 相等的；相当的
recommendation /ˌrekəmen'deɪʃən/	*n.*	the act of telling sb that sth is good or useful or that sb would be suitable for a particular job, etc. 推荐；推荐信

Expressions

1. an ideal job 一份理想的工作

2. job hunting 求职

3. graduation certificate 毕业证

4. recommendatory letters 推荐函

5. London Commercial College 伦敦商学院

6. major in Foreign Trade 主修外贸

7. Universal Trading Company 环宇商贸有限公司

8. feel quite qualified for 感觉挺胜任

9. Alex Hua Tian Hotel 华天酒店

10. a photocopy of my university diploma 我的毕业证复印件

11. technical qualification certificate 专业技术资格证书

12. Beijing Foreign Studies University 北京外国语大学

13. a Network Maintenance Engineer 网络维护工程师

14. Windows 8.1 Operating System Windows 8.1 操作系统

15. Graduate School of Tsinghua University 清华大学研究生院

16. out of question 毫无疑问

Part IV   Practical Writing Tasks

Practice 1 Terms
Match the following business English terms and phrases with their proper Chinese meaning.

1. General Manager	A. 业务经理
2. Marketing Manager	B. 总会计师
3. Chief Engineer	C. 行政助理
4. Executive Director	D. 出纳员
5. Business Manager	E. 总工程师
6. Chief Accountant	F. 电气工程师
7. Electrical Engineer	G. 总经理
8. Marketing Executive	H. 市场部主任
9. Administration Assistant	I. 市场部经理
10. Cashier	J. 行政董事

Practice 2 Fill in the blank with the words and expressions given bellow. Change the form where necessary.

graduated	apply	employee	resume	qualified
interview	diligent	experience	qualifications	convenience

1. I would like to _____ for the position of business assistant to General Manager at your

company.

2. I believe that I am _____ for the position of secretary in your company.

3. I am looking forward to a personal _____ at your convenience.

4. With this practical _____ , I have become more interested in the marketing.

5. My health is excellent and I am _____ and energetic, honest in character and conscientious in work.

6. I feel I have the necessary _____ and experience needed for the position of private secretary to your managing director, advertised in the South China Morning Post.

7. Enclosed in this letter is my _____ . I would be grateful if you would grant me an interview.

8. I would appreciate the opportunity to meet and discuss your requirement at your _____ .

9. With all sincerity, I hope to become an _____ of your honorable company as early as possible.

10. I have just _____ from the College of Law of Beijing University, with a Bachelor's Degree in Law.

Practice 3 Translation

I. Translate the following sentences from Chinese into English.

1. 随函附上我的英文老师的推荐函。

2. 求学中，我曾获奖学金及演讲比赛一等奖。

3. 本人虽刚离开校门，但英文很好。

4. 我希望能和您就广告的职位进一步谈谈。

5. 恳请惠予考虑本人之申请为盼。

II. Translate the following sentences from English into Chinese.

1. I request an interview, and assure you that if appointed, I will do my best to give you satisfaction.

2. Replying to your advertisement in today's issue of the newspaper, I wish to apply for the position in your esteemed firm.

3. Since my graduation from the school two years ago, I have been employed in Tianjin Hotel as a cashier.

4. I have received an English education, and have a slight knowledge of Spanish. I took a Spanish course in college.

5. I wish to assure you that, if successful, I would endeavor to give you every satisfaction.

Practice 4 Practical Writing
Write a letter of application, using the following information.

※ You are required to write a Letter of Application according to the following information given in Chinese

※ 说明：请以李丽霞的名义写一封求职信

李丽霞，24 岁，毕业于北京外国语大学，主修工商管理，各门课程都优良。学过速记与打字，速度分别为每分钟 90 字和 70 字。请为她拟出一份给 ABC 公司的自荐信，希望能在该公司谋得总经理秘书一职。写信的日期为 2014 年 1 月 30 日。

※ Words for Reference:

北京外国语大学 Beijing Foreign Studies University

工商管理 business administration

速记与打字 shorthand and typing

⭐ Part V   Key Sentences for Reference

※ I am writing to apply for the post of salesman advertised in *China Daily* of May 21.

我写信来应聘贵公司在 5 月 21 日的《中国日报》上刊登的招聘销售人员的工作。

※ I can offer your firm a broad skill set with an emphasis on creativity and analysis.

能告知贵公司的是，我具有多种技能，其中以创造力和分析能力尤为突出。

※ I would very much like to meet you to discuss career opportunities.

我将非常高兴与您会面来讨论我此次的就业机会。

※ I know this position requires a sense of responsibility, the courage to face any unexpected challenges as well as necessary skills. But with my education and experience and perseverance,

I'm sure I can perform my duties quite well.

我知道这个职位除了必要的技能之外，还需要有一种强烈的责任感和敢于直面各种挑战的勇气。但我有这样的学历、经历和毅力，相信自己一定能干好。

※ My position as President of the Student Council has helped me develop my leadership and communication skills.

我担任学生会主席，培养了自己的领导能力，提高了自己的交流水平。

※ I would welcome the opportunity to discuss these and other qualifications with you.

我非常乐意与您就这些和其他资格问题进行交谈。

※ I've got the news from the TV that your bureau is to recruit five national public servants this year. After careful consideration, I intend to apply for such a position.

从电视里获悉你局拟招聘五名国家公务员，经过认真考虑后，本人打算参加应聘。

※ I can communicate with foreigners in English in both technical and business fields without any difficulty.

我能毫无困难地用英语与外商进行技术和业务交流。

※ I did well at university; I was one of the top students in the class.

我大学成绩很好，是班上的尖子生。

※ My training, education and personal qualities justify my application for the position.

我所接受的教育和训练，我所具备的个性品质，使我符合该职位的要求，特提出申请。

※ I have passed College English Test Band 6 in my third year at college and got a score of 640 in TOEFL.

我在大学三年级时通过了大学英语六级考试，托福成绩 640 分。

※ I am proficient in shorthand and typewriting and I have attained a speed of 100 and 60 words per minute respectively.

我熟悉掌握速记、打字，速度分别为每分钟 100 和 60 词。

※ As for welfare, my only hope is to enjoy free medical care.

关于福利，本人唯一的希望就是享受免费医疗。

※ I should require that your company provide me with an apartment.

本人要求贵公司给我提供一套单元房。

※ I should be glad to have a personal interview and can furnish references if desired.

如获面谈机会，则甚感高兴。如需推荐函，本人亦可提供。

※ If my qualifications can meet your requirements, please grant me an interview.

如我的资历符合贵公司的要求，请约期面谈。

※ Enclosed are my resume and a letter of recommendation.

附寄简历及推荐信一份。

※ You will find enclosed a photocopy of my ID card, a photocopy of my university diploma, and a photocopy of my technical qualification certificate.

谨随函附上本人的身份证一份，大学毕业证书复印件一份和技术资格证书复印件一份。

※ Thank you for your consideration and I am looking forward to hearing from you soon.

感谢关注，期盼您早日答复。

Business Order
& Confirmations

Learning Objectives

To be proficient in

> understanding knowledge of order & confirmations;
> using key terms, useful expressions and key sentences used in letters of order & confirmations;
> writing a letter of order & confirmations.

Part I   Warming-up Activities

Task 1

Read the following passage about business order & confirmations. Work in pairs to discuss some essential points that an order should contain.

Generally speaking, a procedure of business negotiation in import and export may include:

Enquiry → offer → counter-offer → counter counter-offer → acceptance → contract (order)

An order is a demand to buy an exact amount of goods. It may result from the buyers' acceptance or confirmation of a firm offer made by the sellers or result from the sellers' acceptance or confirmation of a counter-offer made by the buyers.

The essential quality of an order is clarity and accuracy, since its terms and conditions will be used in the sales contract and other relevant documents once the order is accepted.

An acceptance is a fact that the buyers or sellers agree completely to all the terms and conditions in an offer (or a counter-offer as a new offer). If the offer is a firm offer, a deal is concluded after acceptance. If the offer is a non-firm offer, a deal is not concluded until the acceptance is confirmed by the buyers or sellers. In a letter for acceptance or conformation, all the necessary terms and conditions need a further confirmation/check from both sides.

If the terms and conditions in the order are satisfactory, then the seller must indicate his/her acceptance.

If the terms and conditions in the order are not satisfactory, it is impossible for the seller to accept, then the seller may reject the order.

In rejecting the order, it must be written with great care: goodwill, future business, simple, polite and considerate.

Sometimes the goods may run out of stock or due to some other reasons, the seller may offer substitutes.

A repeat order has nothing special in nature. Anything that appears in an initial order may also be contained in a repeat order. But because of previous experience in dealing with the sellers, the buyers are familiar with the sellers' usual practice as well as the details of their products. As a result, a repeat order may be simpler, with many details omitted.

Task 2

Answer the following questions according to the above passage.

1. What is the procedure of business negotiation in import and export?

2. What is an order?

3. What is an acceptance?

Task 3

Match the following business English terms and phrases with their proper Chinese meaning.

1. firm order	A. 试订（单）
2. additional order	B. 追加订单
3. initial order	C. 下订单
4. trial order	D. 接受订单
5. book an order	E. 正式订单
6. accept an order	F. 初次订单
7. close an order	G. 确认订单
8. cancel an order	H. 执行订单
9. execute an order	I. 取消订单
10. confirm an order	J. 决定成交

Part II   Sample Study &Writing Tips

Sample 1 Placing an Order

Dear Sirs,

Subj.Men's Sports Shoes

Thank you for you quotation of March 16, 2013 together with sample shoes you sent to us. Having looked over your sample shoes, we find both the quality and pattern satisfactory and would like to place an order for the following goods:

Commodity: Men's Sports shoes

Size: No. 24, 25, 26, 27 each size 200 pairs

Colors: Red, 50 pairs of different size

   Blue, 60 pairs of different size

   White, 80 pairs of different size

   Black, 60 pairs of different size

Unit price: Australian $ 15 CIF London per pair

We propose "Cash against Documents on Arrival of Goods".We hope we can find a good market for these goods and place further orders with you in the future. Please send us your sales confirmation in duplicate and your prompt attention to this order will be appreciated.

Yours sincerely,

Bruce

Task 1

Discuss the following question: According to the above sample, what aspects should one take into consideration when writing a letter of placing an order?

 # Writing Tips for a Letter of Placing an Order

An order letter should at least contain the following points:

1. name of goods, catalogue No. and sample No.
2. prices of goods, including unit price, total value
3. quality requirement, grade, model name / number and specification
4. quantity of goods
5. origin and material
6. weight, dimensions, color and pattern
7. packing and marking
8. terms of payment
9. delivery requirements, including place, date, mode of transport, etc.
10. documents, such as Bill of Lading, Commercial Invoices, Insurance Policy and special features and others, for example, alternatives if exact goods required are not available.

The following structure can be for your reference in placing an order:

1) Use direct language in the first paragraph to tell the seller of the buyer's intention to place an order.

2) Describe what is being ordered in great detail. Indicate the catalog numbers, sizes, colors, prices, specifications and all other relevant information that will enable the seller to fill the order without any further questions.

3) Close the letter by expressing willingness to cooperate or suggesting future business dealings.

 # Sample 2 Confirming an Order

Task 2

Complete the letter of confirming an order according to the Chinese in the parentheses.

Dear Sirs,

Many thanks for your order dated August 16th for the pure silk prints and welcome you as one of our customers at your end.

1) _____ (我们很高兴确认上述订单) and will try our best to deliver the goods as requested. When the goods reach you, we feel confident that you will be completely satisfied with them.

For goods ordered we usually require payment by a confirmed, irrevocable 2) _____ (信用证) payable by draft at sight upon presentation of shipping documents. Please inform us at an early date 3) _____ (如果你能接受我们的付款条件).

We also enclose our 4) _____ (销售确认书) for your counter-signature.

We hope that our handling of the first order of yours will lead to more business between us and mark a happy working relationship.

Yours sincerely,

Jack Chen

Sample 3 Accepting an Order

 **Task 3**

Compose a letter for accepting an order by using the given information

1. look forward to receiving further orders from you
2. Arrangement for shipment
3. in duplicate
4. please find our Sales Confirmation

> Dear Sir or Madam,
>
>   In reply to your letter of June 18, we take pride in booking your order No. VC54226 for the 180 SAMSUNG Galaxy S4 Note 3. Enclosed 1) _____ No.WA9888 2) _____ , a copy of which is to be returned to us for our file after being countersigned by you.
>
>   Emphasis is to be laid upon the point that the covering letter of credit must be established in our favor through a first-class bank. 3) _____ will be made upon receipt of your L/C. We trust that the shipment will turn out to your satisfaction.
>
>   We appreciate your close cooperation and 4) _____ .
>
> Sincerely yours,
Lucy Chen

Writing Tips for a Letter of Confirming an Order

When confirming an order received, the following structure may be for your reference:

1. Express appreciation for the order received.
2. Assure the buyers that the goods they have ordered will be delivered in compliance with their request. It is also advisable for the sellers to take the opportunity to resell their products or to introduce their other products to the buyers.
3. Close the letter by expressing willingness to cooperate or suggesting future business dealings.

Sample 4 Declining an Order

 **Task 4**

Discuss the following question: According to the following sample, what are the reasons for declining an order?

> Dear Sirs,
>
>   We are in receipt of your letter dated May 11, together with your order sheet for leather gloves. It is necessary for us to express our great thankfulness for your order.

Much to our regret, owing to a shortage of stocks we are unable to fill your order and it will be at least 6 weeks before we get our next delivery. Please feel free to contact us then.

We are looking forward to your future order.

Yours faithfully,

Black Lee

Writing Tips for a Letter of Declining an Order

It is sensible to open the letter in a positive way. Appreciation or pleasure in receiving the order can be stated at the beginning of the letter. When declining an order, detailed and sensible reasons should be provided in order to retain the reader's interest in the writer's products or services. The orders may not be able to be accepted for the following reasons:

1) the goods required are out of stock;

2) prices and specifications have been changed;

3) the buyers and the sellers cannot agree on some terms of the business;

4) the buyer's credit is not in good standing;

5) the manufacturer simply does not produce the goods ordered, etc..

In addition, in order to conclude a deal, the writer usually offers suitable substitutes, makes counter-offers and persuades the buyers to acceptable them. And then end the letter in the way that makes the reader aware of the writer's expectation for future business relations with him.

Sample 5 Placing a Repeat Order

 **Task 5**

Discuss the following question: According to the following sample, what is the structure of the letter of placing a repeat order?

Dear Miss Susan,

Re:SAMSUNG Galaxy S4 Note 3

We are very delighted to inform you that the first order for the 180 SAMSUNG Galaxy S4 Note 3 is quite satisfactory.

As we received many inquiries from our customers at present, and we are sure that we can sell additional quantities in this market. We'd like to place with you a repeat order for another 1,000 SAMSUNG Galaxy S4 Note 3.

As we are in an urgent need of the commodity for the coming sales season,please confirm that you can execute our repeat order before November 11th.

We hope this repeat order is acceptable to you and look forward to your early reply.

Yours sincerely,

David Smith

Writing Tips for a Letter of Placing a Repeat Order

The following structure can be for your reference in writing a letter of placing repeat orders:

1. Open the letter in a positive way, either expressing satisfaction with the fulfillment of previous orders or directly informing the seller of the buyer's intention to place an order.

2. Describe what is being ordered in detail. If any improvement or change of the business conditions is needed, state it clearly in the letter so as to enable the seller to fill the order promptly and accurately without any further questions.

3. Close the letter with a confident expectation of fulfillment of the order.

⭐ *Part III   Vocabulary in Use*

confirmation /ˌkɔnfə'meɪʃən/	*n.*	a statement, letter, etc. that shows that sth. is true, correct or definite 确认；证实
initial /ɪ'nɪʃəl/	*adj.*	happening at the beginning; first 开始的；最初的
cancel /'kænsəl/	*v.*	say that you no longer want to continue with an agreement, especially one that has been legally arranged; call off 取消
execute /'eksɪkjuːt/	*v.*	perform / carry out sth 执行；实行
procedure /prə'siːdʒə/	*n.*	the official or formal order or way of doing sth, especially in business, law or politics 程序；过程；步骤
negotiation /nɪˌɡəuʃi'eɪʃən/	*n.*	formal discussion between people who are trying to reach an agreement 谈判；协商
essential /ɪ'senʃəl/	*adj.*	extremely important and necessary 必要的；重要的
clarity /'klærɪti/	*n.*	the quality of being expressed clearly 清楚
accuracy /'ækʊrəsi/	*n.*	the state of being exact or correct; the ability to do sth skilfully without making mistakes 正确；准确；精确
contract /'kɔntrækt/	*n.*	an official written agreement 合同；契约
document /'dɔkjʊmənt/	*n.*	an official paper or book that gives information about sth, or that can be used as evidence or proof of Sth. 文件；公文
substitute /'sʌbstɪtjuːt/	*n.*	one that takes the place of another; a replacement 代用品；替代物
omit /əu'mɪt/	*v.*	not include (sth); leave out 未包括，不包括（某事物）；省略
quotation /kwəu'teɪʃən/	*n.*	a written statement of exactly how much money something will cost 报价单
commodity /kə'mɔdɪti/	*n.*	a product that is bought and sold 商品
propose /prə'pəuz/	*v.*	put forward for consideration, discussion, or adoption; suggest 提议；建议

duplicate /'dju:plɪkeɪt/	n.	exactly the same as something, or made as an exact copy of something 副本
catalogue /'kætəlɔg/	n.	a complete list of items, for example of things that people can look at or buy 目录；总目
specification /ˌspesɪfɪ'keɪʃən/	n.	a detailed description of how sth is, or should be, designed or made 规格
origin /'ɔrɪdʒɪn/	n.	the place or situation in which something begins to exist 起源；产地
dimension /daɪ'menʃən/	n.	a measurement in space for example, the height, width or length of sth 尺寸；规模；维度
invoice /'ɪnvɔɪs/	n.	a detailed list of goods shipped or services rendered, with an account of all costs; an itemized bill 发票；发货清单
feature /'fi:tʃə/	n.	a prominent or distinctive aspect, quality, or characteristic 特征
alternative /ɔ:l'tə:nətɪv/	n.	choice of two or more possibilities 可能性中的选择；选择对象；选择余地
irrevocable /ɪ'revəkəbəl/	adj.	(formal) that cannot be changed; final 不可撤销的；不能变更的
draft /drɑ:ft/	n.	a written order for money to be paid by a bank, especially from one bank to another 汇票
compliance /kəm'plaɪəns/	n.	action in accordance with a request or command; obedience 服从；听从；遵从；顺从
decline /dɪ'klaɪn/	v.	refuse politely to accept or to do sth 谢绝
retain /rɪ'teɪn/	v.	keep sth; continue to have sth 保持；保留
manufacturer /ˌmænjʊ'fæktʃərə/	n.	a person or company that produces goods in large quantities 厂商；制造者
fulfillment /ful'fɪlmənt/	n.	the act of doing something that you promised or agreed to do 完成；履行
countersign /'kauntəsaɪn/	v.	sign a document that has already been signed by another person, especially in order to show that it is valid 会签；确认

Expressions

1. counter counter-offer 反还盘
2. a firm offer 实盘
3. terms and conditions 条款和条件
4. sales contract 销售合同
5. a non-firm offer 非实盘

6. Cash against Documents on Arrival of Goods 货到后凭单付款

7. sales confirmation 销售确认书

8. in duplicate 一式两份

9. unit price 单价

10. total value 总价值；总价

11. terms of payment 付款条件

12. mode of transport 运输方式

13. Bill of Lading 提货单

14. Commercial Invoices 商业发票

15. Insurance Policy 保险单；保险证书

16. pure silk prints 真丝印花布

17. a confirmed, irrevocable letter of credit 保兑的不可撤销信用证

18. draft at sight upon presentation of shipping documents 出示装运单证时凭即期汇票付款

19. counter-signature 会签

20. in compliance with their request 按照他们的要求

21. out of stock 缺货；已脱销

22. owing to a shortage of stocks 由于库存短缺

⭐ *Part IV   Practical Writing Tasks*

Practice 1 Terms
Match the following business terms and phrases with their proper Chinese meaning.

1. sales confirmation	A. 发货
2. execute shipment	B. 总价
3. out of stock	C. 取消订货
4. in triplicate	D. 会签
5. counter-signature	E. 新订单
6. total value	F. 销售确认书
7. bill of exchange	G. 汇票
8. commercial invoice	H. 无现货
9. cancel an order	I. 一式三份
10. fresh orders	J. 商业发票

Practice 2 Fill in the blank with the words and expressions given bellow. Change the form where necessary.

duplicate	repeat	terms	cancel	promise
accept	fill	stock	payment	order

1. We are very interested in the following goods and have decided to place a trial _____ on the

terms stated in your letter.

2. Enclosed please find our Purchase Order No.188 in _____ , please sign it and return one copy for our counter-signature.

3. For _____ , we can accept L/C 30 days after sight.

4. If the first order proves satisfactory, we shall be glad to place _____ orders with you.

5. At present we have no _____ of the black leather gloves you requested because there is a temporary shortage of the materials for making gloves.

6. Your _____ and conditions are satisfactory and we would like to place an order with you.

7. We hope you will give us opportunity to _____ your order when the goods again become available.

8. We have no choice but to regretfully _____ our order.

9. We regret being unable to _____ your terms of payment and therefore have to return the order to you herewith.

10. We thank you for your order and _____ that your order will be dealt with promptly and carefully.

Practice 3 Translation

I. Translate the following sentences from Chinese into English.

1. 我们认为质量和价格都令人满意。

2. 兹确认按照计划完成交货。

3. 我们遗憾地告知贵方，你方所订货物目前缺货。

4. 请确保货物与样品完全一致。

5. 很高兴接到你方订单，并确认予以接受。

II. Translate the following sentences from English into Chinese.

1. We are sending you our Sales Confirmation No. 168 in duplicate, one copy of which please sign and return for our file.

2. With reference to the goods you ordered, we have decided to accept your order at the same price as that of last year.

3. If you fail to deliver the goods within the specified time, we shall have to cancel the order.

4. As the goods you ordered are now in stock, we will ship them without delay.

5. Our company relies on quick sales, low profits, and a fast turnoff, and therefore we cannot offer long-term credit facilities.

Practice 4 Practical Writing
Write a letter, using the following information.

※ Situational Writing

Read the following situation and write an acceptance letter.

我方乐于接受您6月20日给予我方第5号300双休闲运动鞋，8月装船，旧金山保费、运费在内价，每双25美元的报价。

内附第10号购买确认书，以确定这次交易。

我方已安排银行开立贵方为受益人，金额7500美元的不可撤销信用证，作为这次购货的款项。

请尽快执行此订单，不胜感激。

_____

_____

_____

_____

_____

_____

_____

Part V   Key Sentences for Reference

※ We confirm that deliveries will be made on schedule.

兹确认如期完成交货。

※ We usually only order goods on consignment.

我们通常只能订购寄售的货物。

※ For such a big order, we propose to have the goods dispatched via sea.

对于数量如此大的一批订货，我们打算通过海运。

※ We hope you can dispatch the goods within the stipulated time.

我们希望贵方能在规定期限内发货。

※ We'll do our utmost to ensure the prompt dispatch of the goods to your port.

我们会尽一切努力确保货物准时发运至贵方港口。

※ We confirm that the required items are in stock.

我方确认贵方所需各项产品均有库存。

※ We regret to inform you that the goods you ordered are out of stock at present.

我们遗憾地告知贵方，你们所订货物目前缺货。

※ As the goods you ordered are now in stock, we will ship them without delay.

因贵方所订货物有库存，我们将立即装运。

※ Because the quality of the goods dispatched by you is not in accordance with the contract, we have the right to refuse the goods.

因贵方所交货物与合同不同，我们有权拒收。

※ We enclose herewith our Sales Contract No.123 in duplicate. Please sign and return one copy to us for records.

随函附上我们第 123 号销售合同一式两份，请签退一份供我方存档。

※ As we are in urgent need of the goods, you are requested to effect shipment during August as promised in your offer.

由于我们急需该货，请在你方报盘所承诺的 8 月装运。

※ The relative letter of credit will be opened in your favor soon. Please arrange shipment without any delay upon receipt of the credit.

相关的以你方为受益人的信用证将尽快开出，请收到信用证立即安排装运。

※ Please note that the stipulations in the relative credit should fully conform to the terms in our Sales Contract in order to avoid subsequent amendments.

请注意有关信用证的条款必须与合同条款完全一致，以避免日后修改。

※ We believe that you will fulfill this order with your careful attention.

我们相信你会十分妥善地履行这一订单。

※ We are very pleased to confirm that we have concluded the following transaction with you.

我们很高兴确认与你方达成了以下交易。

※ Enclosed please find our trial order. If the quality measures up to our requirements, we will place large orders before long. Your prompt attention to this order will be appreciated.

随函附上试购订单一份。如果质量达到我们的要求，不久我们就会大量订购。如你方能立即处理该订单，我们不胜感激。

※ Thank you for your order No.123. We accept it and will dispatch the goods early June.

谢谢贵方 123 号订单，我们接受此订单，并将于 6 月初交货。

※ We are pleased to confirm your order for the T-shirts on the following terms.

我们很高兴确认贵方按以下条件订购 T 恤的订单。

※ The price you quoted is workable. Therefore we have cabled you our acceptance.

我们认为贵方报价可行，已去电表示接受。

※ We would be grateful if you would sign the contract and return one copy to us for our record as soon as possible.

如贵公司能尽快签署合同并寄回一份供我方备案，我们将不胜感激。

※ Thank you very much for your cooperation and hope that this may be the beginning of long and friendly relationship between us.

十分感谢贵方的合作。希望此次合作成为我们双方长期友好关系的开端。

Business Letters of Packing & Shipment

Learning Objectives

To be proficient in

➢ understanding knowledge of packing & shipment;
➢ using key terms, useful expressions and key sentences for business letters of packing & shipment;
➢ writing a letter of insurance packing & shipment.

Part I Warming-up Activities

Task 1

Work in groups to discuss the functions of cargo packaging.

Task 2

Match the following terms in the left column with their Chinese equivalences in the right column.

1. shipping company	A. 装运通知
2. shipping agent	B. 装运标志
3. shipping instruction	C. 装运港
4. shipping advice	D. 装船日期
5. shipping documents	E. 轮船公司，船务公司
6. shipping mark	F. 货运代理人
7. shipping container	G. 舱位；船位
8. shipping port	H. 船运集装箱
9. shipping space	I. 装运单据
10. shipping date	J. 装运指示；装运须知

Task 3

Read the following passage about international goods transportation and goods shipment, then answer the question below:

What are the types of transportation in international trade?

International Goods Transportation and Goods Shipment

In international trade, the international goods transportation and goods shipment are two of the important components of the international trade. Only through transporting, can the goods be transported from the seller's country to the buyer's country.

After signing the selling and buying contract, the seller should ship the goods to the buyer according to the time, place and way of shipment stipulated in the contract. In carrying out the procedures of foreign trade, the concept of time should be paid great attention to.

The fields in which foreign trade is involved are extensive, the transportation lines are long. The links and procedures are numerous, so the foreign traders must be equipped with fundamental knowledge of the international cargo transportation and shipment.

Only in this way can the deliberate consideration be offered to the problems of the cargo transportation and the terms of transportation may be worked out completely, definitely and reasonably, thus making sure of the successful effecting of the contract.

Kinds of Transportation in International Trade are as following:

1. Ocean Marine transportation

2. Rail transportation

3. Air transportation

4. Highway transportation

5. River transportation

6. Postal transportation, etc.

Part II   Sample Study &Writing Tips

Sample 1 Asking for Details of Packing

Dear Sir or Madam,

Re: Details of Packing

Thank you for your suggestion of November 17, 2014 for the packing manner of the goods under our Order No. 618. Our customers are very satisfied with the packing of the above-mentioned order.

Meanwhile, our customers wish to know the details of packing, namely,

1. In what manner will the goods be packed so that the packing looks attractive and helpful to the sales?

2. What effective measures will you take to prevent the goods from moisture and rain?

3. What kind of packing materials will be used to make the packing strong enough to withstand rough handling, prevent the goods from damage, and make it convenient to handle during the course of loading and unloading?

We hope that the result of packing turns out to be satisfactory for our customers.

We look forward to your early reply.

Yours sincerely,

Jack Smith

Task 1

Discuss the following question: According to the above sample, what aspects should one take into consideration when writing a packing letter?

Writing Tips for Letters regarding packing

In order to pack goods to withstand long voyages, buyers usually write to give explicit packing instructions. The seller can describe in detail to the buyer his customary packing of the goods concerned and also indicate clearly that he may accept any required packing at the expense of the buyer. The buyer can inform the seller of any formerly unexpected requirements or fears about the packing. Any changes regarding packing stipulated in the contract should be mutually discussed and determined before shipment. In such letters, be sure to provide clear, definite and concrete instructions instead of general and lacking details.

A packing letter is composed of the information as follows:

1. The order number or contract number on the subject line

2. The purpose of the letter, i.e. negotiation on packing

3. Customary packing of the goods concerned or packing requirements such as packing material, packing way and quantity as well as packing mark, packing fee and so on

4. Reasons for using this kind of packing

5. Your expectation and desire.

Sample 2 Shipping Advice

Dear Sir or Madam,

<u>Re: Shipping Advice</u>

We wish to inform you that the machines you ordered June this year under Contract No. 416 is on board S.S. "East Wind" which will sail tomorrow from New York to Dalian.

In order to assure you of the goods' reaching you in good condition, all of them were packed in special container. We wish you to unpack and examine them immediately on arrival. Any complaints as to damage should be notified to us and the shipping company within ten days.

Enclosed please find the following copies of shipping documents:

1. one non-negotiable copy of the bill of loading

2. commercial invoice in duplicate

3. one copy of the certificate of guarantee

4. one copy of the certificate of quantity

5. one copy of the insurance policy

We hope the goods will reach you in time and in sound conditions to meet with your full satisfaction.

Sincerely yours,

Linda

 **Task 2**

Discuss the following question: According to the above sample, what aspects do the shipping documents usually include?

 # Sample 3 Shipment Packing and Shipping Marking

 **Task 3**

Complete the letter of shipment packing and shipping marking according to the Chinese in the parentheses.

Dear Sir or Madam:

Re: Shipment Packing and Shipping Marking

　　We are writing to you to invite your attention to our order No. 322 covering 1,000 sets of chinaware for dinner service made in Liling, Hunan. The goods ordered should be delivered before December 1 1) _____ (如合同规定). We are sorry to say that up till now we still have not heard from you any news of delivery of these goods. Please pay attention to the delivery date and 2) _____ (尽早安排发货).

　　In addition, the chinaware are easily to be broken and are, especially, not capable of withstanding the rough handling. Therefore taking good care of well packing is of great importance for reducing the losses in transporting. It is necessary for you to pack the goods in strong wooden cases bedded with foamed plastics for protection from being broken.

　　3) _____ (至于运输标志), we wish you to do it according to our requirements as follows:

　　1. Mark the cases correctly and distinctly with our initials in a triangle, under which comes the destination port with Contract number.

　　2. For the sake of precaution, please mark "Fragile" and "Handle with care" on the outer packing.

　　We hope that the packing will be strong enough to stand rough handling and long voyage 4) _____ (在运输过程中).

Sincerely ours,

Betty

 # Sample 4 Urging Shipment

 **Task 4**

Compose a letter to urge shipment by using the given information.

1. inform us of the delivery time and effect shipment
2. meet the demand of the selling season
3. We are very anxious to know about the shipment
4. As the season is rapidly approaching

Dear Sirs,

　　1) _____ of our Order No. 717 covering 1,000 dozen cotton shirts. We sent you 10 days ago an irrevocable L/C—expiration date being October 12th.

2) _____ , our buyers are badly in need of the goods. The contracted time of delivery rapidly falling due, it is imperative that you 3) _____ as soon as possible in order to enable the goods to arrive here in time to 4) _____ .

Please take good consideration of our urgent request and let us have your favorable reply. Your immediate effectuation of the shipment will be most appreciated.

We thank you in advance for your cooperation.

Sincerely yours,Helen

Sample 5 Informing Shipment

Dear Sirs:

Re: Your Sales Confirmation No. A168 Covering 1000 Dozen cotton shirts

We have the pleasure to acknowledge the receipt of your letter dated August 18th related to the above subject.

In reply, we are pleased to inform you that the confirmed, irrevocable L/C No. 618, amounting to $2,000 has been opened this morning with the Bank of Beijing. Upon receipt invoice please arrange shipment of the goods booked by us as soon as possible.

We would like you to send the goods to Shanghai port. Should this trial order prove satisfactory to our customers, we can assure you that repeat orders in large quantity will be placed.

Your close co-operation in this respect will be highly appreciated and we are looking forward to your shipping advice.

Yours sincerely,

Bruce Lee

Task 5

Discuss the following question: According to the above Samples 2-5, what aspects should one take into consideration when writing letters regarding shipment?

Writing Tips for Letters regarding shipment

Shipment is the process of transporting commodities and cargo by land, air or sea.Letters regarding shipment are usually written for the following purposes:

➢ To urge an early shipment

➢ To amend shipping terms

➢ To give shipping advice

➢ To dispatch shipping documents.

In international trade the buyer sometimes sends the shipping instructions (including shipping requirements) to the seller. Sometimes the buyer will write to the seller for informing the seller of effecting shipment in time in case of shipment delay. After the shipment of the goods, the seller will send the buyer the shipping advice to inform the buyer the related shipment details.

The letters of shipment usually involve the information as follows:

1. The date and number of the order and contract

2. The shipped goods and the names of commodities and their quality and value

3. The way of shipment and the name of carrying vessel

4. The date and number of bill of lading

5. The name of the shipping port / loading port and the destination port

6. The estimated time of departure and arrival

7. A list of relevant shipping documents bill of loading, seaway bill, airway bill, railway bill, cargo receipt, commercial invoice, certificate of origin, certificate of quality, packing list, insurance policy and survey report and so on.

⭐ Part III Vocabulary in Use

retail /'ri:teɪl/	v.	sell in small quantities directly to consumers 零售
transit /'trænsɪt/	n.	the process of being moved or carried from one place to another 运输；运送
transparent /træn'spærənt/	adj.	allowing light to pass through so that objects behind can be seen clearly 透明的
transaction /træn'zækʃən/	n.	a business deal or action, such as buying or selling something 交易
corrugated /'kɔrəgeɪtɪd/	adj.	in the shape of waves or folds, or made like this in order to give something strength 波纹状的
ingot /'ɪŋgət/	n.	a solid piece of metal, especially gold or silver, usually shaped like a brick 锭，铸块
identification /aɪˌdentɪfɪ'keɪʃən/	n.	the process of showing, proving or recognizing who or what someone/something. is 识别；辨认
abbreviation /əˌbri:vi'eɪʃən/	n.	a short form of a word, etc. 缩写
consignee /ˌkɔnsaɪ'ni:/	n.	the person that something is delivered to 收件人；代销人
corrosive /kə'rəusɪv/	n.	a substance having the capability or tendency to cause corrosion 腐蚀剂
radioactivity /ˌreɪdiəuæk'tɪvɪti/	n.	the sending out of radiation (= a form of energy) when the nucleus (= central part) of an atom has broken apart 放射性
inflammable /ɪn'flæməbəl/	adj.	that can catch fire and burn easily 易燃的
fragile /'frædʒaɪl/	adj.	easily broken or damaged 易碎的
conspicuous /kən'spɪkjuəs/	adj.	easy to see or notice; likely to attract attention 显眼的；出众的；显著的

| withstand /wɪð'stænd/ | v. | be strong enough not to be hurt or damaged by extreme conditions, the use of force, etc. 经得起；经得住；耐（磨、穿） |
| expiration /ˌekspɪ'reɪʃən/ | n. | the ending of a fixed period of time 期满；截止 |

Expressions

1. safe and sound 安然无恙
2. pilferage-proof 防盗的
3. push sales 推销
4. household consumer goods 家庭消费品
5. conclude a transaction 成交
6. barcode 商品条码
7. trade mark 商标
8. brand name 商标；商标名称
9. place of original 原产地
10. Colgate toothpaste 高露洁牙膏
11. a corrugated box 瓦楞纸箱
12. crude oil 原油
13. ingot aluminum 铝合金锭
14. indicative marks 指示标记
15. warning mark 警示标志
16. terms of transportation 运输条款
17. Ocean Marine transportation 远洋海运

Part IV   Practical Writing Tasks

Practice 1 Terms
Match the following business English terms and phrases with their proper Chinese meaning.

1. shipment terms	A. 装运时间
2. time of shipment	B. 装运港
3. port of shipment	C. 装船通知
4. port of destination	D. 装运条款
5. mode of transport	E. 目的港
6. freight	F. 运输方式
7. optional port	G. 运费
8. shipping advice	H. 选择港
9. bill of lading	I. 装船指示
10. shipping instructions	J. 提单

Practice 2 Fill in the blank with the words and expressions given bellow. Change the form where necessary.

requested	precaution	withstand	advice	customer
packing	considerations	shipping	damage	shipment

1. With regard to the _____ for the above order, the goods should be packed in tin-lined water-proof woolen bale.

2. We hope that the result of packing turns out to be satisfactory for our _____ .

3. We have noted that you have taken careful _____ on the packing of our goods.

4. Now that the shipping date is approaching, we should have your shipping _____ .

5. Our customers are in urgent need of the goods and any delay in _____ our ordered goods will undoubtedly bring our customers inconvenience.

6. The packing must be strong enough to _____ rough handling.

7. We suggest that you reinforce your packing in order to reduce _____ to the minimum.

8. For the sake of _____ , the cartons must be secured with metal bands.

9. Upon receipt of our L/C, please arrange _____ of the goods which we ordered without delay.

10. As _____ , we will inform you of the date of dispatch immediately upon completing shipment.

Practice 3 Translation

I. Translate the following sentences from Chinese into English.

1. 我们已将货物装上直达轮，将于本月 20 日驶往你港。

2. 请分三批平均装运我方货物，每两个月一批。

3. 副本的海运单据已于昨日空邮你方。

4. 请务必使包装适合海运。

5. 请放心，我们会根据合同装运。

II. Translate the following sentences from English into Chinese.

1. The shipping containers can be opened at both sides for loading and unloading at the same time. They are watertight and airtight and can be loaded and locked at the factory.

2. We take this opportunity to inform you that we have loaded the above goods on board S/S Victoria, which is due to sail for your port tomorrow.

3. It has to be stressed that the shipment must be made within the prescribed time limit, as a further

extension will not be considered.

4. We trust you will see to it that the order is shipped within the stipulated time, as any delay would cause us no little inconvenience and financial loss.

5. Enclosed please find one set of the shipping documents covering this consignment, which comprises: the commercial invoice, bill of lading, packing list, and certificate of origin and insurance certificate.

Practice 4 Practical Writing

Write a letter, using the following information.

※ no news of shipment
※ in urgent need of the machines
※ impossible to extend L/C again
※ L/C expires on 20th August
※ Expectation of shipping advice

_____

_____

_____

_____

_____

_____

_____

_____

Part V Key Sentences for Reference

※ As this article is fragile, please case it into durable packing.
这种物品易碎，请以耐用包装来装箱。

※ We require the inner packing to be small and exquisite to help sales and the outer packing to be light and strong to be easy to carry.
我方要求内包装小巧而精美以有助于销售，外包装轻便而坚固以易于搬运。

※ Each carton is lined with a water-proof material and secured by strapping, preventing the contents from damage through rough handling.
每个纸箱内衬防水材料，用带子加固，防止由于粗鲁装卸使货物受损。

※ We suggest that you reinforce your packing in order to reduce damage to the minimum.

我方建议贵方加固包装以便把破损降低到最低限度。

※ For the sake of precaution, the cartons must be secured with metal bands.

为了预防起见，纸板箱必须用钢带保护。

※ For the sake of precaution, please mark "Fragile" and "Handle with care" on the outer packing.

为了预防起见，请在外包装上注明"易碎"和"小心轻放"字样。

※ Please line the containers with waterproof materials so that the goods can be protected against moisture.

为了以防货物受潮，请用防水材料装衬容器。

※ The full details regarding packing and marking must be strictly observed.

有关包装和唛头的详细规定，都要严格执行。

※ This kind of packing is quite popular for this product in the world market.

此种包装是这种产品国际市场上的流行包装。

※ The goods are packed five pieces to a carton.

货物每5件装一纸箱。

※ Upon receipt of our L/C, please arrange shipment of the goods which we ordered without delay.

收到信用证后，请立刻装运我方所订货物。

※ Please deliver the cases as soon as possible to the American Pier for shipment.

请立即将箱装货物运往美国码头装运。

※ The dispatch of the remaining 50 cases of goods with transshipment via Hong Kong at the most possible speed facilitate the dispatch of the goods to our customers on time.

尽快装运剩余的50箱货物，允许在香港转运，有利于我们按时将货物发运到客户手中。

※ We are pleased to inform you that the first lot consignment has been duly dispatched.

我们高兴地通知贵方第一批货物已按时发运。

※ We have the pleasure of informing you that your order is now ready for shipment, and we await your instructions.

我们很高兴地通知你方，贵方所订货物备妥待运，等候贵方指示。

※ The goods are being prepared for immediate delivery and will be ready for shipment tomorrow.

该货物可以立即交付，准备明天装船。

※ Please permit the consignment under L/C DE186 to be transshipped because there is no direct liner available.

因无船直达，请允许将信用证DE186项下货物转船。

※ The shipment has arrived in the port in good condition.

货物已抵达码头，情况良好。

※ The goods has been shipped on S.S. "London" for transshipment at Dalian.

货已装上"伦敦"号汽船，在大连转船。

※ Shipment is to be made during August to October in three equal lots.

在8月至10月间货物分三次平均装运。

※ We arrange the goods to be shipped in two lots during August to October.

我们安排8月至10月分两批装运货物。

Business Complaints, Claims & Settlement

Learning Objectives

To be proficient in

➢ understanding knowledge of complaints, claims and settlement of claim;

➢ using key terms, useful expressions and key sentences for letters of complaints, claims and settlement of claim;

➢ writing a letter of complaints, claims and settlement of claim.

⭐ Part I   Warming-up Activities

🐧 Task 1

Work in groups to discuss as many common causes as you can for customer complaints and claims.

🐧 Task 2

Work in pairs and discuss how to deal with complaints.

🐧 Task 3

Read the following passage about business complaints, claims & settlement of claim and answer the questions:

Business relationships do not always run smoothly. Complaints take place now and then. Claims are usually raised by buyers for great loss. The buyer mainly complains about the products in quality, damage, packing, shortage and the wrong or delayed delivery. However, sellers may also raise claims against buyers for non-establishment of L/C or breach of contract, etc.

In international trade, claims do not happen in every transaction but often occur. Sometimes when the loss is not serious, the party suffered the loss may not lodge a claim for compensation. Instead he writes a complaint to call the other party's attention to avoiding this matter happening again.

Every business should have a customer complaint handling policy. The better the policy, the better customer relations will be. Most customers who have had a complaint handled appropriately, respectfully, and with resolution, will make a point to return the favor with returned business.

1. What aspects does the buyer mainly complain about the products?

2. For what reason may sellers also raise claims against buyers?

⭐ Part II   Sample Study &Writing Tips

Sample 1 Complaint about Poor Packing

Dear Sir or Madam,

I am writing with reference to Order No. 1688 which we received last week.

When we checked the computer we noticed some damage to the case and when we turned it on, it did not work. It seems that the computer was not packed properly or tested before dispatch. Would you please let me know whether or not you would be willing to send me a new computer and if I should arrange to return the damaged one to you? Please let us know what you intend to do in this matter.

We look forward to your early reply.

Yours sincerely,

Jack Smith

 **Task 1**

Discuss the following question: According to the above sample, what contents does a complaint letter consist of?

Sample 2 A Claim for Poor Packing

 **Task 2**

Complete the letter of a claim for poor packing according to the Chinese in the parentheses.

Dear Sirs,

A Claim for Poor Packing

1) _____ (我们很遗憾通知您) that the wool covered by our Order No. 1196 and shipped per S/S Queen arrived in such an unsatisfactory condition that 2) _____ (我们不得不向贵方提出索赔). It was found upon examination that nearly 20% of the packages had been broken, obviously 3) _____ (由于包装不良). The only recourse in consequence, was to have them repacked before delivering to our customers, which inevitably resulted in extra expenses amounting to $686. We trust you understand the inconvenience caused by it and meanwhile 4) _____ (期待贵方对此作出赔偿).

We should like to remind that special care be taken in your future deliveries for prospective customers are liable to misjudge the quality of your goods by the poor packing.

Yours faithfully,

Kate Smith

Sample 3 A Claim for Damage of Goods

Dear Sir or Madam,

Re:Our order No. AJ-18

The chinaware you supplied to our order of 2nd January, 2014 was delivered by the shipping company this afternoon. The 120 cartons containing the goods appeared to be in perfect condition .But when I unpacked them with great care, I regret to report that 10 cartons of chinaware were badly cracked .

We trust you can understand that we expect thecompensation for our damaged goods.

We look forward to your early reply.

Yours sincerely,

Tom Smith

 **Task 3**

Discuss the following question: According to the above three samples, what strategy should one take into consideration when writing a claim letter?

Sample 4 A Claim for Inferior Quality

**Task 4**

Compose a letter of a claim for inferior quality by using the given information.

1. a copy of Survey Report for your attention

2. The quality of the goods is much inferior to the sample

3. Thank you for the prompt delivery

4. take the goods back and replace them with goods of the quality we ordered

> Dear Sir or Madam,
>
> **Re: Claim on 1,200 shirts size 39**
>
> Our No. 168 concerning 1,200 shirts size 39 has been duly received. 1) _____
>
> Upon unpacking the consignment, we found, to our great disappointment, that the goods are not of the quality we ordered. 2) _____ , on which we approve the order. As evidence, we are enclosing 3) _____ .
>
> We are not in a very awkward situation, because our clients, who have been very strict about the quality, are very impatient to take delivery of the goods. Therefore, we have no choice but to ask you to 4) _____ .
>
> We look forward to your early reply.
>
> Yours sincerely,
Mary Lee

Writing Tips for Complaint Letters

A complaint letter requests some sort of compensation for defective or damaged merchandise or for inadequate or delayed services. The essential rule in writing a complaint letter is to maintain your poise and diplomacy, no matter how justified your gripe is. Avoid making the recipient an adversary.

1. Identify early the reason you are writing — to register a complaint and to ask for some kind of compensation. Avoid leaping into the details of the problem in the first sentence.

2. State exactly what compensation you desire, either before or after the discussion of the problem or the reasons for granting the compensation.

3. Provide a fully detailed narrative or description of the problem. This is the "evidence".

4. Explain why your request should be granted. Presenting the evidence is not enough: state the reasons why this evidence indicates your request should be granted.

5. Suggest why it is in the recipient's best interest to grant your request: appeal to the recipient's sense of fairness, desire for continued business, but don't threaten. Find some way to view the problem as an honest mistake. Don't imply that the recipient deliberately committed the error or that the company has no concern for the customer. Toward the end of the letter, express confidence that the recipient will grant your request.

Sample 5 Settlement of a Claim

Dear Sir or Madam:

Re: Settlement of Your Claim

We acknowledge the receipt of your letter dated December 20, 2013, claiming for a shortage in weight on the consignment of polished rice.

On examination, we found that some bags were broken during transit and breakage resulted in the shortage. We therefore accept your claim as tendered and enclose our Check No. 1618 for US $ 600.

We are very sorry for the trouble caused to you and would like to assure you that we'll make great efforts to avoid any recurrence like this in our future dealings with you.

Yours sincerely,

Michael Chen

Task 5

Discuss the following question: According to the above sample, how should one write a reply to a complaint or claim letter?

Writing Tips for Adjustment Letters

Replies to complaint letters, often called letters of "adjustment," must be handled carefully when the requested compensation cannot be granted. Refusal of compensation tests your diplomacy and tact as a writer.

Some suggestions:

1) Begin with a reference to the date of the original letter of complaint and to the purpose of your letter. If you deny the request, don't state the refusal right away unless you can do so tactfully.

2) Express your concern over the writer's troubles and your appreciation that he has written you.

3) If you deny the request, explain the reasons why the request cannot be granted in as cordial manner as possible. If you grant the request, don't sound as if you are doing so in a begrudging way.

4) If you deny the request, try to offer some partial or substitute compensation or offer some friendly advice.

5) Conclude the letter cordially, perhaps expressing confidence that you and the writer will continue doing business.

Part III   Vocabulary in Use

claim /kleɪm/	*n.*	demand for a sum of money (as insurance, compensation, a wage increase, etc.) 索赔（作为保险金、 赔偿、 增薪等）

breach /briːtʃ/	*n.*	an action that breaks a law, rule, or agreement 违反（法律、法规或协议）
lodge /lɔdʒ/	*v.*	present (a statement, etc.) to the proper authorities for attention 向负责部门提出（某事）
compensation /ˌkɔmpən'seɪʃən/	*n.*	something, especially money, that sb gives you because they have hurt you, or damaged sth that you own; the act of giving this to sb 补偿；赔偿金
prospective /prə'spektɪv/	*adj.*	likely to become or be 预期的；可能要成为的
crack /kræk/	*v.*	break without dividing into separate parts 裂开
consignment /kən'saɪnmənt/	*n.*	a quantity of goods that are sent or delivered somewhere 所托运的货物；代销货物
defective /dɪ'fektɪv/	*adj.*	having a fault or faults; not perfect or complete 有缺陷的；欠缺的
poise /pɔɪz/	*n.*	a calm and confident manner with control of your feelings or behavior 镇定；镇静
diplomacy /dɪ'pləuməsi/	*n.*	skill in dealing with people without upsetting them 交际手段；策略
justified /'dʒʌstɪfaɪd/	*adj.*	having a good reason for doing sth 有正当理由的；情有可原的
gripe /graɪp/	*n.*	a complaint about sth 抱怨
adversary /'ædvəsəri/	*n.*	a person that sb is opposed to and competing with in an argument or a battle 敌手；对手
grant /grɑːnt/	*v.*	give someone something or allow them to have something that they have asked for 给予；允许；授予
polished /'pɔlɪʃt/	*adj.*	Having the husk or outer layers removed. Used of grains of rice 碾净的（谷壳或外层被去除了的）
breakage /'breɪkɪdʒ/	*n.*	an object that has been broken 破坏；破损
recurrence /rɪ'kʌrəns/	*n.*	an occasion when something that has happened before happens again 重现；复发
cordial /'kɔːdiəl/	*adj.*	sincere and friendly 诚恳的；亲切的；友好的
begrudging /bɪ'grʌdʒɪŋ/	*adj.*	giving or expending with reluctance 吝惜的；勉强给予的

Expressions

1. breach of contract 违约；违反合同
2. lodge a claim for compensation 提出赔偿要求；索赔
3. with reference to 关于
4. result in 导致

5. amounting to 总计为；相当于

6. prospective customers 潜在客户

7. be in perfect condition 在完美的条件下；完好无损

8. to our great disappointment 使我们感到非常失望的是

9. in a very awkward situation 在一个非常尴尬的境地

10. acknowledge the receipt of 告知收到

11. adjustment letter 海损理算书，（保险业中）要求赔偿评定信，理算书

Part IV   Practical Writing Tasks

Practice 1Terms

Match the following business English terms and phrases with their proper Chinese meaning.

1. damaged goods   A. 重量证明

2. faulty goods   B. 破损证明

3. delayed delivery   C. 货物受损

4. false documents   D. 次货

5. Survey Report   E. 检验证书

6. Certificate of Inspection   F. 保险单

7. Invoice   G. 发票

8. Insurance Policy   H. 延期交货

9. Weight Certificate   I. 单据有误

10. Damage Report   J. 检验报告

Practice 2 Fill in the blank with the words and expressions given bellow. Change the form where necessary.

refund	apologize	compensation	sample	delivery
damaged	settle	investigate	complaints	standards

1. Much to our regret, we have found that one of the cases of your consignment is badly _____ .

2. We have no choice but to ask you to ship replacement for the claim and _____ the survey charge of US$ 180.

3. We trust you will promptly _____ this claim.

4. In order to settle the claim, we will immediately send a representative to _____ the matter.

5. We _____ for the trouble caused to you and assure you that we will give you a satisfactory answer.

6. If our party was at fault, the _____ will be made at once.

7. The customers make _____ about the quality of the computers supplied by you.

8. Your goods are not up to the _____ commonly accepted.

9. On examination we find that the consignment does not correspond with the original _____ .

10. We are now in a very awkward situation because our customers are very impatient to take _____ of the goods.

Practice 3 Translation

I. Translate the following sentences from Chinese into English.

1. 这件商品的价钱与它的价值很不相称。

2. 关于你最近的来信，我对你的投诉非常抱歉。

3. 我们已将您的索赔报告递交给了保险公司。

4. 我方不得不要求你方承担这一损失。

5. 我们向您保证以后一定会为您提供更加优质的服务。

II. Translate the following sentences from English into Chinese.

1. We regret to tell you that the goods specifications you sent us are not in conformity with that stipulated in the contract.

2. You will be responsible for the shortages, defects or anything which don't conform to the contract.

3. Should you not agree to accept our proposal, we would like to settle by arbitration.

4. If the inspection confirms the accuracy of your estimate, generous compensation will be allowed at once.

5. We apologize sincerely once again for this error and the inconvenience it brought to your company.

Practice 4 Practical Writing
Write a letter, using the following information.

※ You live in a room in college which you share with another student. You find it very difficult to work there because your roommate always has friends visiting. He / She has parties in the room and sometimes borrows your things without asking you.

※ Write a letter to the Accommodation Officer at the college and:

※ 1) ask for a new room next term,

※ 2) you would prefer a single room,

※ 3) explain your reasons.

_____

_____

_____

_____

_____

_____

_____

⭐ Part V   Key Sentences for Reference

※ As the goods are not in conformity with the L/C, we cannot help filing a claim against you.

由于这批货物与信用证不符，我们只好向你方提出索赔。

※ We checked some of the items and found they were in damaged condition.

我们检查了部分产品，发现它们已严重受损。

※ After checking the goods against your invoice, we discovered a considerable shortage in number.

经过核对发票，我们发现数量短缺很多。

※ Your shipment of goods has been found short in weight by CCIB (China Commodity Inspection Bureau，中国商品检验局) for which we regret.

经中国商品检验局检验后发现对方出运的货物短重，对此我方非常遗憾。

※ We have to ask for a compensation to cover (deal with) the loss incurred as a result of the inferior quality of the goods concerned.

我们不得不提出索赔要求，以补偿由于货物质量低劣而蒙受的损失。

※ If you cannot deliver the goods within ten days, we'll reluctantly turn this matter to our attorney.

如果在 10 日内不能送达货物，我们不得不付诸法律。

※ I hereby inform you that I am lodging a formal complaint with your company.

特此通知贵方，我公司将正式投诉贵公司。

※ As your complaint does not agree with the results of our own test, we suggest that another thorough examination be conducted by you to show whether there is any ground for claim.

由于你方投诉与我方检验结果不一致，我方建议你方再彻底检验一次，以证明是否有索赔的理由。

※ We regret to inform you that the goods received are not in accordance with our orders.

我们很遗憾地通知你们，所收货物与我们所订货物不符。

※ On examination, we found that the goods do not agree with the original sample.

检查发现，货物跟原来样品不一致。

※ This is the maximum concession we can afford. Should you not agree to accept our proposal, we would like to settle the case by arbitration.

这是我们所做的最大的让步，如果您不接受我们的建议，我们想由仲裁解决此事。

※ We find no grounds to compensate for the loss you claimed for.

我方没有理由赔偿贵方索赔的损失。

※ In support of our claim, we are sending you a survey report issued by CCIB.

兹寄去中国商品检验局检验报告一份，作为我方索赔的依据。

※ We may compromise, but the compensation should, in no case, exceed $ 500, otherwise, this case will be submitted to arbitration.

我方可以让步，但赔偿不得超过 500 美元，否则将提交公断。

※ We trust that you will settle this claim as soon as possible.

我们希望贵方尽快理赔。

※ If you cancel the claim, we'll try to make you a reasonable compensation in our future deals.

如果你方取消索赔，我们将在今后的交易中给你方做出补偿。

※ We shall appreciate your prompt attention to the adjustment of this claim.

如能从速办理索赔，我们不胜感激。

※ It would not be fair if the loss be totally imposed on us, as the liability rests with both parties. We are ready to pay 50% of the loss only.

责任应由双方承担，如果所有损失都强加在我们身上是不公平的，我方只愿支付 50% 的损失。

※ As it is a matter concerning the insurance, we hope that you will refer the claim to the insurance company or their agent.

鉴于这是一个涉及保险的问题，希望你方向保险公司或其代理商提出索赔。

※ We are ready to compensate your loss if we should accept responsibility for this claim.

如果我方应该承担此次索赔的责任，我方愿意对你方损失进行赔偿。

Answers to Exercises

Unit 1

Part II

Task 3

1. This contract requires your signature by October 10th.

2. Thank you for your check for US $30,000.

3. I'm sorry that I can't do as you wish.

Task 5

1. appreciated   2. informed   3.grateful

Part IV

Practice 1

1. C   2. F   3. G   4. A   5. H   6. E   7. J   8. B   9. D   10. I

Practice 2

| 1. Concerning | 2. regret | 3. help | 4. enclose | 5. available |
| 6. attractive | 7. reception | 8. samples | 9. planning | 10. informed |

Practice 3

I.

1. We have noticed in your letter that the damages to five chairs in shipment were found.

2. We hope to receive the amount due by the end of this month.

3. We hope you are satisfied with our goods, and look forward to receiving your future orders.

4. We apologize again for any inconvenience.

5. Please inform us what special offer you can make for us .

II.

1. 你方若能够送一些材料的样品以便于我方检验产品的质地，我方将不胜感激。

2. 我方比较了你方和其他供应商所给出的价格，贵公司的产品价格比美国和德国的供应商所给的价格高了将近 5 个百分点。

3. 请你方在 11 月底之前确认你方将执行订单，以便于我方能够为销售旺季做好准备。

4. 我方很抱歉你方要求的货物无法获取，因为它们已脱销。

5. 你方能否处理所有的装运手续和保险，并发给我方提货单，商务发票和保险证书 / 凭证的副本？

Practice 4

Dear Sirs,

    We are interested in your various types of digital cameras. We introduce ourselves as one of the largest importers of electric goods in China and have been in this line for over ten years. We expect to establish business relations with you with keen interest. Please sends us a full range of illustrated catalogues and samples. We will appreciate it very much if you will quote us the lowest price with earliest delivery.

    We look forward to your early reply.

Yours faithfully

Unit 2

Part II

Task 2

1) Attention   2) memos   3) prohibited   4) intra   5) apply   6) employees

Task 3

1) gained valuable experience

2) In particular,

3) it is time to further develop

4) acceptable to the company

5) thank you for your support

Part IV

Practice 1

All department managers;

HR manager

October 28th;

Schedule a meeting

Room 202

Practice 2

1. remind   2. adopt   3. board   4. cost   5. response   6. free   7. appreciate   8. reference   9. propose   10. benefit

Practice 3

I.

1. Please note that the Health and Safety Inspectors will be visiting us tomorrow.

2. The company has found it necessary to cut expense.

3. If anybody would like to take holidays together with the Spring Festival holidays, please inform your manager in advance.

4. Members of staff who cycle to work leave their bicycles behind the office building.

5. I have been informed of the meeting and would ask for an overhead projector for the meeting.

II.

1. 双方确认一方并未因本备忘录从另一方获得该方任何知识产权（包括但不限于版权、商标、商业秘密、专有技术等）或针对该知识产权的权利。

2. 除非按照法律规定有合理必要，未经另一方事先书面同意，任何一方不得就本备忘录发表任何公开声明或进行任何披露。

3. 对本备忘录进行修改，需双方共同书面同意方可进行。

4. 中美双方签署了反垄断、反托拉斯的合作备忘录。

5. 如蒙在 2009 年 4 月 1 日前填妥表格并送回办公室，将不胜感激。

Practice 4

Memo for the Month of English Program

To: The Management of the University

From: The Student Union

Date: May 20, 2008

Subject: Regarding the Month of English Program

The Student Union plans to hold a Month of English Program. The program involves a series of English-related activities, aiming at improving the students' English skills and promoting the students' interests in learning English. The program is scheduled to officially start on June 1 and lasts the whole month.

Unit 3

Part II

Task 1

1) Organized by the Student Union

2) basketball match

3) postgraduates

4) basketball court

Task 3

Notice

The swimming pool of Jiangsu University will be open to the public from June 15 this year.

Time: 8:00 a.m. — 10:00 p.m.

Fee:RMB 3 Yuan / hr for an adult

RMB 2 Yuan / hr for a child

Please have swimming suits with yourselves.

The President's Office

June 12, 2012

Part IV

Practice 1

1) are preparing to

2) With the efforts of

3) ranked

4) a number of activities

5) are welcome

Practice 2

1. Owing to	2. branch	3. orders	4. express	5. lead to
6. notify	7. behalf	8. advantage	9. guarantee	10. confidence

Practice 3

I.

1. I inform you that I have now moved my factory to the above address.

2. Having established ourselves in this city, we take the liberty of acquainting you of it.

3. Our business will be turned into a limited company on the 1st of May.

4. Through these lines, we inform you that they may send you many orders.

5. Admission by tickets only.

II.

1. 我以微软公司为名开设总代销店，特此奉告。

2. 本公司将于 8 月 1 日改为私营企业，特此奉告。

3. 兹定于本月 21 日我们在本市以凯特·金的名义开设绸缎棉布行，特此奉告。

4. 我方已在本市开设贸易和总代理店，特此通知。同事，恳请订购。

5. 我将以斯通公司的名义营业，特此奉告。

Practice 4

You won't want to miss this!

INTERNATIONAL FOOTBALL MATCH

China vs Australia

Place: Capital Gymnasium

Time: 3:30 p.m. June 28,2008

Please apply at Reception Office for tickets

Come and cheer for them

Unit 4

Part I

Task 1

1. 飘柔　2. Swatch　3. 七喜　4. Mercedes-Benz

Part II

Task 2

1) Awaits　2) be　3) manor　4) elegant

Task 3

1) overlooking　2) course　3) Close　4) access　5) study

Part IV

Practice 1

1. E　2. G　3. A　4. J　5. I　6. B　7. C　8. L　9. K　10. H　11. F　12. D　13. P　14. O　15. M　16. N

Practice 2

1. With reference to　2. advertisement　3. In reply to　4. apply for　5. Personnel

6. fill　7. position　8. considered　9. writing　10. hearing from

Practice 3

I.

1. Advertising techniques are changing from stagnant ads to interactive tableaus.

2. Advertisers create modern art with a message.

3. Short videos can be effective ads for your business.

4. The latest advertising trends use humor, creativity and urgency to appeal to potential customers and speak with them directly.

5. Go beyond the ordinary and watch store traffic soar.

II.

1. 至于说到广告，你可以选择各种不同方法来释放商品信息。

2. 在零售企业，广告是营销组合中的一个重要工具。但是如果没有合理利用的话，将会耗费很多的时间和金钱。

3. 了解一些时下流行的各种广告模式的不同之处是很必要的。

4. 用收音机和有线电视做一些商业广告可以达到更广泛的宣传目的，让更多的人知道你的产品。

5. 这类广告的费用比较高，如果投放的季节对的话，还是具有一定的合理性的。但是，在做广告预算的时候，你可能需要加上产品自身的生产成本。

Practice 4

The genius Galanz Home Appliance Company has come up with a new model Microwave ovens -EB-3190EG. It can cook the food with amazing speed by heating the food. Furthermore its convection facility provides fans and a certain "airflow" circulation that cooks the food by using much less electricity. It can bake, broil, cook, re-thermalize and warm the food effectively which makes it be the best oven available in the market that provides the users with delicious, tasty and fast cooked foods.

Basic functions of this new model:

1. Halogen grill

2. Electronic operation with LED display

3. 10microwave power levels

4. 90minutes time setting

5. Auto menu & auto defrost function

6. Child lock

7. Quick start key

Following are some of the other advantages of microwave convection oven:

There are heating and cooling switches, which heat and cool the food perfectly. The nutrients are preserved and the actual taste of the food also remains same. The oven operates at much lower temperature and leads to 20% decrease in cooking time compared to other ovens.

If you still don't have an excellent microwave oven like this, then hurry up and get yourself this oven to provide wonderful dishes to your family and friends.

Unit 5

Part I

Task 1

1. E   2. A   3. D   4. B   5. C

Part II

Task 1

1) lnviting   2) held   3) Great Wall   4) attend   5) look forward to

Task 2

1) secretary   2) attend the reception   3) would be grateful   4) dress formally   5) meet all your expenses

Task 3

1. I am writing to extend/convey my heart-felt thanks/sincere appreciation/gratitude to you for…

Task 4

My true gratitude is beyond words. Thank you again.

Part IV

Practice 1

1) assisting   2) expressing   3) add   4) appreciation   5) helpful   6) looking forward to   7) greeting

Practice 2

1. inviting   2. accept   3. specific   4. Fair   5. sorry   6. pleased   7. contact   8. request   9. service   10. solving

Practice 3

I.

1. On 7th July, we will host an evening of celebration in honor of the retirement of Mr. Wang, president of ABC Company.

2. You are cordially invited to attend the celebration at Huzhou Hotel No.290 Kangtai Road, Huzhou, at 7:00 pm on April 5th, 2009.

3. Mr. Wang has been the President of ABC Company since 1999. During this period, ABC Company expanded its business extensively.

4. Now it's our opportunity to thank him for his years of exemplary leadership and wish him well for a happy retirement.

5. Please join us to say Good-bye to Mr. Wang.

II.

1. 张忠良夫妇恭请 Ng Lai Si 女士光临女儿张颖和董志强先生的婚礼。

2. 我们十分荣幸地邀请您参加这个会议。

3. 感谢您一直以来对本公司的关心和支持，使公司得以业务蓬勃发展。

4. 诚邀请您在下周四，5月15日来我公司进行考察指导交流，并赴本公司的庆典午宴。

5. 如您认为能接受邀请，请务必通知我您抵达这里的日期和时间。

Practice 4

April 20,2006

Dear sir,

We are preparing to celebrate the 20th anniversary of our company. With the efforts of all our staff, our company is now ranked as one of the five leading companies in the same field both in scope and profits. To celebrate our achievements, we will hold a number of activities.

We would like to invite you, our regular business partner, to attend our celebrating ceremony and activities. The ceremony will take place at Lotus Hotel, at 9:18 a.m. on May 28. There will also be a reception at 10:30. We hope you will be able to attend.

Looking forward to your reply.

Yours sincerely,

Li Wei

Unit 6

Part I

Task 1

1. 非正式报告   2. 正式报告   3. 便函体报告   4. 书信体报告

5.可行性报告　　　6.事故报告　　　7.调查报告　　　8.进度报告

9.公差报告　　　10.建议报告

Part II

Task 1

1) The general manager has asked me to compile a report on the possibility of working flextime

2) Staff who had recently moved or who had lived far away from the firm for some time

3) The greatest volume of telephoned requests for information and advice

4) The least busy period was from 3 to 5 p.m.

5) All staff must be in the premises between 10:30 a. m. and 3:00 p.m.

Task 2

1) In May, we have scheduled one advanced course and two basic courses

2) this training is on a voluntary basis

3) The manual will be ready for distribution by May 10

Part IV

Practice 1

1. E　　2. I　　3. J　　4. D　　5. H　　6 . G　　7 . F　　8. B　　9. C　　10. A

Practice 2

1. objective　　　2. recommends　　　3. access　　　4.negative　　　5. modes

6. distributed　　　7. collective　　　8. presented　　　9. distributed　　　10. aspects

Practice 3

I.

1. This report describes the training courses that have been devised to effect this goal.

2. In view of the importance of these training courses to our corporate goals, I recommend the following suggestions.

3. These points call for further understanding and discussion and arrangements will be made for another meeting.

4. The purpose of this visit was to find out whether it would be possible for ABC to provide cabinets to us at a fixed price for a certain period.

5. I will draft a copy of the meeting summary, fax it to ABC and ask them to make changes and then send us a copy by return fax.

II.

1. 7 月上旬做的 50 份谈话调查显示购物城的购物环境在许多方面不能满足顾客的需要。

2. 因此设施和服务需要改进。最明显的是大堂、洗手间、通风设施、试衣间和收款服务。

3. 此次走访获得了成功，与永康公司的会谈与磋商就几个重要问题达成了一致意见。

4. 我已要求工人检查了全部屋顶，并警告所有人以防止此类事件的再次发生。

5. 调查问卷的主要发现就是大多数工作中的母亲需要下午 3:30 以后有空闲时间。

Practice 4

To: Jacob Prior, General Manager

From: Emily King, Director of Training Department

Date: May 4, 2014

Subject: Investigation of the possibility of adopting English Program for senior employees

Introduction

The general manager has asked me to compile a report on the possibility adopting English Program for senior employees. 200 questionnaires were issued, of which 196 were returned. The needs and requests were collected and recommendations were listed.

Findings

A. Staff Needs:

Only 24% of the stuff members were satisfied with their English and 90% of the senior employees expressed their keen needs of improving their English proficiency.

B. Staff Preferences:

1. 70% of them desired to improve their listening and speaking ability, while 40% writing skills.

2. 79% of the staff would prefer to take class after work at five in the afternoon at weekdays, while 21% at weekends.

3. 98% of the staff would take class delivered by foreign teachers.

Recommendations

Business English program by New Oriental could be adopted, for it aims to improve English listening and speaking ability of in-service staff. Both evening and weekend class are available for stuff members to choose.

Unit 7

Part I

Task 1

1. China International Fair for Investment and Trade(Xiamen) 投洽会

2. Standard Chartered 渣打银行

3. Bank of China 中国银行

4. China Chamber of International Commerce (CCOIC) 中国国际商会

5. China High-tech Fair (CHTF) (Shenzhen) 高交会

6. Citibank 花旗银行

7. China Import and Export Fair (Canton Fair) 广交会

Part II

Task 1

we shall be pleased to enter into business relations with you at an early date

Part IV

Practice 1

1. F   2. C   3. E   4. J   5. G   6. B   7. D   8. I   9. A   10. H

Practice 2

1. credit	2. line	3. consummated	4. represented	5. inquires
6. exclusively	7. attention	8. delivery	9. possibilities	10. Expanding

Practice 3

I.

1. On the recommendation of your Chamber of Commerce, we have learned with pleasure the name and address of your firm.

2. If your corporation does not import the goods mentioned above, please give this letter to the firm who may be concerned.

3. Please let us have your specific inquiry if you are interested in any of the items listed in the catalogue. We shall make an offer promptly.

4. We understand that you are exporters of Chinese Arts & Crafts. We, therefore, are taking liberty of writing you.

5. We are enclosing a catalogue and a price-list for your reference, so that you may acquaint yourselves with some of the items we handle.

II.

1. 如蒙航寄目录册和价格表将不胜感激。

2. 我方在贸易界有良好的关系，对这类产品的进口富有经验。

3. 非常高兴收到贵方的来信，我们将认真考虑有可能促进贵我双方合作的任何建议。

4. 我们对和贵公司建立商贸关系非常感兴趣，旨在向贵公司供应所需的电器和电子产品。

5. 从我国驻贵国大使馆商务参赞处获悉，贵公司是电器和电子产品的主要进口商之一。

Practice 4

Dear Sirs,

On the recommendation of British Chamber of Commerce, we have learned with pleasure the name and address of your firm. As one of the leading exporters to UK, we have excellent producing line of children's garments. We sincerely hope we would enter into business relations with you at an early date.

If you are interested in our products, please let us know your reference. Illustrated catalogue and price-list will be air-mailed against you specific inquiries.

We look forward to hearing from you soon.

Your Sincerely,

Jane Fox

Unit 8

Part II

Task 3

1) I had mistakenly typed in the wrong item number

2) The revised PO is attached

3) undue inconvenience

Part IV

Practice 1

1. Business-to-Business

2. Business-to-Consumer

3. Business-to-Government

4. Consumer-to-Consumer

5. Electronic Commerce

Practice 2

1. prompt	2. estimated	3. inconvenience	4. quote	5. confirm
6. detailed	7. transfer	8. instructions	9. currently	10. Expedite

Practice 3

I.

1. Please refer to the e-catalogue enclosed.

2. I shall feel obliged by a reply at your earliest convenience.

3. We are writing to enter into business relations with you on a basis of mutual benefits and common developments.

4. As the price of raw material often changes, the offer valid period is not very long.

5. Thank you very much for your E-mail enquiry and now we feel pleased in attaching you our price list.

II.

1. 我方可以立即发货，望在下周来传真订货。

2. 一旦此货可以供应，我们将以传真通知贵方。

3. 请通过电子邮件或传真确认收到此订单。

4. 确认订单后我们立即把您作为受益方开不可撤销信用证。

5. 正如您在报价单中所表明的那样，我们希望立即出库发货。

Practice 4

Dear Sir,

We saw your ad for your new products in the February issue of Clean Room Magazine, and we are very interested in them. Considering we are expanding the market in China, we would like to see your brochure of these new products.

I shall feel obliged by a reply at your earliest convenience.

Yours,

Jimson Frank

Unit 9

Part I

Task 1

1. 国际商会	2. 国际货币基金组织
3. 联合国贸易和发展组织	4. 经济合作与发展组织
5. 世界贸易组织	6. 经济互助委员会（经互会）
7. 东南亚国家联盟	8. 国际投资银行
9. 亚洲太平洋经济合作组织	10. 国际金融组织

Part II

Task 1

1) absented from duty

2) taken a very serious note

3) Any employee's absenting without prior sanction

4) In case of any emergency

5) submit the leave application form immediately

Task 2

1) We are pleased to know that you are particularly interested in our "Spring" series, which is our leading series of this year.

2) In order to encourage you to lay in a stock of this new design, we'd like to give you a special discount of 10% on all orders of more than MYM20,000.

Part IV

Practice 1

1. Depreciate 降价促销

2. Draw a lottery 有奖促销

3. Discount 打折优惠

4. Contest 竞赛促销

5. Taste the free 免费品尝促销

6. Trial promotion 试用促销

7. Give as a present 赠送促销

8. Exhibit 展览促销

9. Offer special service 特别服务

10. Members Rewards Program 会员积分

Practice 2

1. stock   2. illustrated   3. absolutely   4. locality   5. promising

6. recommend   7. requirements   8. place   9. trial   10. subject

Practice 3

I.

1. This product is the result of our latest technology.

2. We are most gratified that you have selected our products for years.

3. By virtue of its superior quality, this item has met with a warm reception in most European countries.

4. Being moderate in price, excellent in craftsmanship, and unique in design, our products are very popular with the young.

5. As this product is now in great demand, we would advice you to work fast and place an order with us as soon as possible.

II.

1. 您可以免费试用两周我们新开发的手机。

2. 该产品受到国内外消费者的赞誉和青睐。

3. 我方认为，购买这个产品对你方市场试探性的销售是很有好处的。

4. 我方给贵方订单提供优惠折扣，期望发展双方的贸易关系。

5. 我们相信上述条款可为贵方接受，盼贵方最后订单。

Practice 4

Dear Mr. Farmer,

We are sure that you would be interested in the new model of our packaging machine, which is moderate in price, excellent in craftsmanship and unique in design. By virtue of its superior quality, this item has met with a warm reception in experts home and abroad.

Considering our long-term cooperation, we offer you a 30-day trail of our new product. If you are interested, please contact with us.

packaging@eee.com

Telephone number:010-85726666

Fax number: 010-85726668

Email:packaging@hotmail.com

Postal Address: Dawang Road 11, Chaoyang District, Beijing.

Unit 10

Part II

Task 2

1) We have instructed the Royal bank of Scotland to open a credit for ￡ 60,000 in your favor, valid until 30th December.

2) The credit will be confirmed by the Bank of China, Suzhou Branch, who will accept your draft on them at sight for the amount of your invoice.

Task 3

1) we found some discrepancies

2) at 60 days after sight

Task 4

1) we are supposed to deliver the goods next week

2) the validity of your L/C to 30th August

Part IV

Practice 1

1. G   2. H   3. A   4. F   5. C   6. B   7. D   8. E

Practice 2

1. shipment	2. deferred	3. punctual	4. acceptance	5. issued
6. accordance	7. confirm	8. promptly	9. delete	10. extend

Practice 3

I.

1. Please act promptly and let us have your cable reply the soonest possible.

2. As a rule, we only accept confirmed irrevocable letter of credit payable by draft at sight.

3. However, we regret to have found that there are certain clauses which do not conform to those of the contract.

4. We regret to inform you that we did not receive your L/C covering the above Sales Confirmation till today.

5. Kindly notify the buyers that we shall make an amendment in the L/C freight collect instead of C&F New York.

II.

1. 尽管我方多次提醒，贵方至今尚未开立信用证。

2. 我们坚持凭不可撤销的即期信用证付款。

3. 开即期信用证是我方对我们所有客户的要求。

4. 我们同意将即期信用证付款方式改为即期付款交单。

5. 因信用证的有效期为 5 月 31 日，希望将其有效期延长至 6 月 10 日。

Practice 4

> We wish to acknowledge receipt of your L/C No. 101, covering your order for 1000 dozen of Children's garment. we found some discrepancies. Please amend you L/C as follows:
>
> 1). the terms of payment should be "D/P at sight" instead of "L/C at sight".
>
> 2) the port of destination should be "Toronto" instead of "Montreal".
>
> 3) the unit price should be "$100" instead of "¥100".
>
> Your early fox amendment to the L/C will be highly appreciated.
>
> Sincerely yours,
>
> Jepson

Unit 11

Part I

Task 1

1. 中国人保控股公司   2. 中国人民财产保险股份有限公司

3. 中国人寿保险（集团）公司   4. 中国人寿保险股份有限公司

5. 中国再保险（集团）公司   6. 中国财产再保险股份有限公司

7. 中国人寿再保险股份有限公司   8. 中国大地财产保险股份有限公司

9. 中国保险（控股）有限公司   10. 太平保险有限公司

Part II

Task 2

1) we are pleased to inform you

2) we are making arrangements to ship the order by S. S. Dongfeng

3) If you have any further question, please feel free to contact me anytime

Task 3

1) 2   2) 3   3) 4   4) 1

Part IV

Practice 1

1. J   2. D   3. F   4. G   5. H   6. E   7. A   8. I   9. B   10. C

Practice 2

1. terms and conditions   2. insurance policy

3. coverage   4. approval

5. insured   6. response

7. shipping advice   8. cover

9. contact   10. claim

Practice 3

I.

1. We are pleased to receive your letter requesting us to insure your goods.

2. This is an insurance policy with extensive coverage.

3. For CIF transactions, we usually effect insurance for 110% of the invoice value against risks.

4. We have insured at 110% of the invoice value.

5. The extra premium for additional coverage, if required, shall be borne by the buyer.

II.

1. 在发货前，我们希望确认贵公司是否已经为即将运送到我们公司的货物上保险。

2. 我们很高兴收到通知，贵公司由上海运往伦敦的一批雕像交由我公司承保。

3. 根据您 10 月 16 日来信要求保险，我们已经向平安保险公司为贵公司的货物投保了一切险。

4. 我们知道按照贵方一般惯例，你们只会按发票价格另加 10% 投保，因此额外保险费由我方负责。

5. 按照我方惯例，只保基本险，按发票金额 110% 投保。

Practice 4

Dear Sir / Madam,

Re: Your Order No. 123 for 5,000 Cartons of Silk Blouses

We have received your letter of December 16, requesting us to insure the captioned goods for an amount of 120% of the invoice value.

Although it is our usual practice to take out insurance for 110% of invoice value, we'd like to comply with your request for getting cover for 120% of the invoice value. But the extra premium will be for your account.

We are looking forward to your early reply.

Sincerely yours

Paul Johnson

Unit 12

Part I

Task 1

In business negotiations there are four key links: inquiry, offer, counter-offer and acceptance.

Part II

Task 3

1) there's a ready market for our products

2) In compliance with your request

3) If you find this offer is acceptable

Task 4

1) Commodity   2) Quantity   3) Quality   4) Price   5) Shipment   6) Payment

Part IV

Practice 1

1. F   2. D   3. A   4. J   5. H   6. C   7. I   8. B   9. E   10. G

Practice 2

1. enquire	2. reasonable	3. payment	4. discount	5. credit
6. quotation	7. quote	8. order	9. offer	10. confirmation

Practice 3

I.

1. If your price is reasonable, quality satisfactory and delivery acceptable, we will send you large orders.

2. This offer is firm / valid for fifteen days.

3. We can offer you a quotation based upon the international market.

4. It's no easy job for us to persuade the customers to buy your products at this price.

5. Our price is reasonable, compared with that in the international market.

II.

1. 请贵公司尽快惠寄电脑的最新价目表和带有图片的商品目录，并给予最优惠的报价。

2. 若你方的质量好且价格适合我方市场，我们愿考虑与你方签署一项长期合同。

3. 由于我方可能长期大量订货，相信你方将会做出某些特殊的让步。

4. 我方产品物美价廉，我们坚信你方能接受我方 6 月 16 日的报盘。

5. 不是我们有长期的业务关系，我们是不愿意以这个价格报实盘的。

Practice 4

A Letter of Inquiry

December 30, 2013

Dear Mr. Peter Kevil,

Subj. Jet Printer

We are very much interested in the jet printers manufactured by your HP Company. We'd like to know your prices and after-sale services. If you send us your lowest quotations and provide good services, we would consider placing an order.

Looking forward to your prompt reply.

Sincerely yours,

David Johnson

A Letter of Reply

January 2, 2014

Dear Mr. David Johnson,

Thank you for your inquiry of June 30. We're grateful to know that you are interested in our jet printers.

We enclose our latest price list together with a copy of our catalog. We're glad to tell you that we are always ready to provide you with good service. If you place regular orders for large quantities, we can offer you special discount.

We are looking forward to your first order.

Yours truly,

Peter Kevi

Unit 13

Part II

Task 2

1) I am writing to apply for the position of senior receptionist

2) I have three years' work experience

3) I have excellent computer skills

4) I look forward to hearing from you

Task 4

1) 3   2) 2   3) 1   4) 4

Part IV

Practice 1

1. G   2. I   3. E   4. J   5. A   6. B   7. F   8. H   9. C   10. D

Practice 2

1. apply	2. qualified	3. interview	4. experience	5. diligent
6. qualifications	7. resume	8. convenience	9. employee	10. graduated

Practice 3

I.

1. Enclosed you will find a letter of recommendation from my former teacher of English.

2. At school I won a scholarship and the first prize in a speech contest.

3. I have just left school, but have a good knowledge of English.

4. I look forward to talking further with you about the advertised position.

5. I hope that you will be kind enough to consider my application favorably.

II.

1. 恳请惠予面试之荣。如蒙录用，本人必竭尽所能，为贵公司服务，以符厚望。

2. 拜读贵公司在今日（报纸）上广告，特此备函应征贵公司该职位。

3. 两年前离校后，在天津酒店担任出纳员。

4. 本人接受英文教育，同时略通西班牙文。大学时，我修了西班牙文。

5. 如蒙不弃，惠予录用，本人将尽力服务，使诸事满意。

Practice 4

A Letter of Application

January 30,2014

Dear Sir or Madam,

I'm writing to apply for the post of secretary to General Manager in your company.

As you will see from the enclosed V.V., I am 24 years old. I graduated from Beijing Foreign Studies University in 2010. I majored in Business Administration. I had received very good grades in each course. In addition, I also have received the training of shorthand and typing. I am able to take shorthand at 90 words per minute and type 70 words a minute. I have two years' experience in Business Administration and am looking for greater challenges and increased responsibility.

I would be very grateful for the opportunity to meet and could be available at any time for an interview.

Yours sincerely,

Li Lixia

Unit 14

Part I

Task 3

1. E   2. B   3. F   4. A   5. C   6. D   7. J   8. I   9. H   10. G

Part II

Task 2

1) We are very delighted to confirm the mentioned order

2) letter of credit

3) if you can accept our payment terms

4) Sales Confirmation

Task 3

1) 4   2) 3   3) 2   4) 1

Part IV

Practice 1

1. F   2. A   3. H   4. I   5. D   6. B   7. G   8. J   9. C   10. E

Practice 2

1. order   2. duplicate   3. payment   4. repeat   5. stock   6. terms   7. fill   8. cancel   9. accept   10. promise

Practice 3

I.

1. We find both the quality and price satisfactory.

2. We confirm that deliveries will be made on schedule.

3. We regret to inform you that the goods you ordered are out of stock at present.

4. Please see to it that the goods are exactly the same as our sample.

5. We are pleased to receive your order and confirm acceptance of it.

II.

1. 现寄上第 168 号销售确认书一式两份，请签署并寄回一份供我方存档。

2. 关于你方订购货物，我们决定按去年价格接受你方订单。

3. 如果你们不能在规定的时间内交货，我们将取消订单。

4. 因贵方订货尚有存货，我们将尽快装运。

5. 我们公司依靠薄利多销、快速周转，所以不能提供长期信贷。

Practice 4

> Gentleman:
>
> We are glad to accept your offer of June 20 for 300 pairs No.5 at US MYM25 a pair CIF San Francisco for August shipment.
>
> Enclosed is our Purchase Order No.10 to confirm this transaction.
>
> In order to cover the amount of this purchase, we have arranged with our bankers for an Irrevocable Letter of Credit amounting to US MYM7500 to be opened in your favor.
>
> Your prompt execution of this order will be very much appreciated.

Unit 15

Part I

Task 2

1. E   2. F   3. J   4. A   5. I   6. B   7. H   8. C   9. G   10. D

Part II

Task 3

1) as stipulated in the contract

2) arrange the shipment as early as possible

3) As to the shipping marking

4) in the course of transportation

Task 4

1) 3   2) 4   3) 1   4) 2

Part IV

Practice 1

1. D   2. A   3. B   4. E   5. F   6. G   7. H   8. C   9. J   10. I

Practice 2

1. packing   2. customer   3. considerations   4. advice   5. shipping

6. withstand   7. damage   8. precaution   9. shipment   10. requested

Practice 3

I.

1. We have shipped the goods on the direct steamer which will sail for your port only around the 20th this month.

2. Please ship the goods in three equal lots, each every two months.

3. The duplicate shipping documents were airmailed to you yesterday.

4. Please see to it that the packing is suitable for a long sea voyage.

5. Please rest assured that we'll make shipment as contracted.

II.

1. 船运集装箱能两头开启供同时装货及卸货，船运集装箱是防水和密封的，在厂内可以装货，也可锁上。

2. 我们借此通知你方，我们已经把上述货物装到维多利亚轮上，该船于明天驶往你港。

3. 我们强调货物会在规定时间内装运，进一步的迟延是不可能的。

4. 我方相信你方会注意订单需在规定时间内发运一事，因为任何耽搁都会引起我们许多不便和经济损失。

5. 现附上这批货物的装运单据一套，包括商业发票、提单、装箱单、原产地证明和保险凭证。

Practice 4

> Dear Sirs,
>
> Re: Contract no. 12345
>
> Referring to our previous letters and cables we wish to call your attention to the fact that up to the present moment no news has come from you about the shipment under the captioned contract.
>
> As you have been informed in one of our previous letters, the users are in urgent need of the machines contracted and are in fact pressing us for assurance of an early delivery.
>
> Under the circumstances, it is obviously impossible for us to again extend L/C No. 12345, which expires on 20th August, and we feel it our duty to remind you of this matter again.
>
> As your prompt attention to shipment is most desirable to all parties concerned, we hope you will let us have your telegraphic shipping advice without further delay.
>
> Yours faithfully,
> ……

Unit 16

Part II

Task 2

1) We are regretful to inform you   2) we have to lodge a claim against you

3) due to insufficient packing   4) expect your compensation for this

Task 4

1) 3   2) 2   3) 1   4) 4

Part IV

Practice 1

1. C   2. D   3. H   4. I   5. J   6. E   7. G   8. F   9. A   10. B

Practice 2

1. damaged   2. refund   3. settle   4. investigate   5. apologize

6. compensation   7. complaints   8. standards   9. sample   10. delivery

Practice 3

I.

1. The price of this commodity does not match its value at all.

2. In reference to your recent letter, I was sorry about your complaint.

3. We have reported your claim to the insurance company.

4. We have to ask you to undertake this loss.

5. We assure you that we will provide higher quality services in the future.

II.

1. 很遗憾，你方运来的货物规格与合同不符。

2. 货物有短少、缺陷或任何与合同规定不符的情况，将由你方负责赔偿。

3. 如果贵方不接受我方建议，我们想由仲裁解决。

4. 如果检查结果确认您方正确，您将立刻获得慷慨赔偿。

5. 对此失误而对贵公司造成的不便，本公司再一次致以诚挚的歉意。

Practice 4

Dear Sir or Madam,

I am writing to express concern regarding accommodation. I would prefer to move into a single room next semester, as I find the present sharing arrangement inconvenient.

I must explain that the reason for my dissatisfaction is my roommate's inconsiderate behavior. For one thing, his friends are constantly visiting him; for another, he regularly holds noisy parties.

To solve this difficulty, I hope to draw the attention of the authorities concerned. I am sure you will agree that the only solution for me is to move into a room of my own. Therefore, I would be grateful if you could find a single room for me, preferably not in the same building but as near to the college campus as possible.

Sincerely yours

Mary

References

[1] 张东昌. 实用商务英语教程 [M]. 北京：高等教育出版社，2009.

[2] 火树钰. 国际商务英语 [M]. 北京：清华大学出版社，2009.

[3] 伊辉春. 外贸英语信函写作 [M]. 北京：高等教育出版社，2011.

[4] 浩瀚，陈淑萍. 商务英语写作实战实例 [M]. 北京：北京航空航天大学出版社，2011.

[5] 肖付良，高平，刘燕. 新编实用英语写作 [M]. 北京：中国人民大学出版社，2013.

[6] 李飞. 国际商务英文写作实务 [M]. 北京：机械工业出版社，2011.

[7] 廖英. 实用英语应用文写作 [M]. 长沙：中南大学出版社，2003.

[8] 张燕如，徐益. 应用英语写作 [M]. 北京：外语教学与研究出版社，2007.

[9] 滕美荣，许楠. 外贸英语函电 [M]. 北京：首都经济贸易大学出版社，2005.

[10] 廖英. 实用外贸英语函电 [M]. 武汉：华中科技大学出版社，2003.

[11] 隋思忠. 外贸英语函电 [M]. 大连：东北财经大学出版社，2004.

[12] 齐智英. 商务英语函电 [M]. 北京：机械工业出版社，2004.

[13] 贾琰. 实用商务英语文函写作 [M]. 北京：化学工业出版社，2004.

[14] 刘庆华. 实用英语 [M]. 北京：科学出版社，1999.

[15] 方宁，王维平. 商务英语函电 [M]. 杭州：浙江大学出版社，2004.

[16] 步雅芸. 商务英语写作 [M]. 北京：北京大学出版社，2010.

[17] 赵伟华，张艳敏. 实用商务英语写作 [M]. 大连：大连理工大学出版社，2003.